GRILLING
with
FOIL PACKETS

DELICIOUS ALL-IN-ONE RECIPES FOR QUICK MEAL PREP, EASY OUTDOOR COOKING, AND HASSLE-FREE CLEANUP

CYNDI ALLISON

Published in the US by:
ULYSSES PRESS
PO Box 3440
Berkeley, CA 94703
www.ulyssespress.com

ISBN: 978-1-64604-025-4
Library of Congress Control Number: 2019951418

Printed in the United States
10 9 8 7 6 5 4 3 2 1

Acquisitions editor: Bridget Thoreson
Managing editor: Claire Chun
Project editor: Tyanni Niles
Editor: Phyllis Elving
Proofreader: Renee Rutledge
Front cover design: Rebecca Lown
Cover photographs: grill © Panptys/shutterstock.com; beef © Joshua Resnick/shutterstock.com; chicken © Africa Studio/shutterstock.com; corn, shrimp, fruit, and potatoes © Cyndi Allison
Production: what!web @ whatdesign.com

TABLE OF CONTENTS

INTRODUCTION

I can still remember the magic of my first "hobo pack." I was attending a Girl Scout day camp at a local park, and one of our activities was to cook our own lunch. My experiences in the kitchen had been less than stellar, and at home I had been relegated to dishwasher duty after catching Pop-Tarts on fire. So, it was a complete head rush when I ripped into the foil pack I'd created with hamburger, potatoes, and onion and caught the enchanting scent of a five-star meal. Okay, my foil packet was not a masterpiece, but it was mine, and it was delicious.

My days of foil-packet cooking faded into the background as I went off to college, married, and gave birth to two sons. As a military family, we were constantly packing and unpacking our belongings, and much of our cooking was on the fly as we enjoyed overseas duty stations. Once back stateside, I discovered that cooking on the stove was "uncool," as one of my boys was fond of labeling drudgery, but grilling was a party. I quickly remastered myself as a frequent-flyer grill master, and my sons jumped on the barbecue bandwagon.

It was a natural leap to volunteer to help my sons' Boy Scout troop with outdoor cooking. We quickly moved beyond foil-wrapped hamburger and potatoes to all sorts of meats and vegetables cooked over the flames. And, of course, we had to have desserts. Is it even possible to become an Eagle Scout (both boys earned the rank) without eating a ton of s'mores?

Family and friends constantly asked me for recipes and directions for grilling and pit cooking, so I started my *Barbecue Master* blog, which garnered a lot of hits and opportunities to talk outdoor chef-ery. At one point I had thirty grills on my porches and tucked into garage and basement spaces. We grilled so much that one of my sons called from college to ask me if hamburgers could be cooked indoors, in a pan, on a stove. His friend had suggested frying hamburgers for dinner, and he was certain that burgers could only be made outdoors—on the grill or in hobo packs. You never know what you're going to learn in college. But I'll wager that outdoor hamburgers still taste better!

Though I love all outdoor cooking techniques, I'll always have a soft spot for foil-packet cooking. And while I still love ground beef with veggies, I've found that almost anything edible can be cooked in aluminum foil. Playing with foil and fire has been an adventure, and I hope that my ideas put a sparkle in every reader's eye just as that first little foil pack did for me as a young girl. It's great to find magic in something so simple and tasty, and it's even more fun to build on the basics to create little works of culinary art.

HISTORY OF FOIL-PACKET COOKING

I can visualize a caveman or woman stuffing food in grape leaves or packing clay around a prized morsel before placing it in the fire. Of course, we have no real way of knowing when cooking became part of culture, but scientists estimate that humans started experimenting with cookery 1.9 million years ago. Foil-packet cooking, of course, doesn't date back to Neanderthal times. Early meal packets made of parchment paper were popularized in France, and the concept crossed the ocean to the United States in the mid-1800s. French immigrants to New Orleans made quite a splash with fish cooked "en papillote" (in parchment).

Tin foil was developed for industrial use in the nineteenth century. The shiny paper was used mainly for packaging things like cigarettes and chocolate, since the metal wrap kept out light and moisture.

Tin foil was rather stiff, and it tended to leach a metallic taste into foods, so entrepreneurs worked to find better solutions. Aluminum foil was developed in Switzerland in 1910 and soon became the favored wrap for chocolate bars. In 1913, aluminum foil became the packaging for Life Savers candy, chewing gum, and candy bars in the U.S. Companies could press-roll three times as much aluminum as tin per pound of metal, so the shift to aluminum was cost effective.

Foil packaging got a boost in the U.S. when Richard Reynolds founded the U.S. Foil Company in 1919 to supply facilities in Kentucky with commercial foil. After several expansions, the company took aluminum foil to the general public in 1947 for home kitchen use under the name Reynolds Wrap. The product became increasingly popular, since it was nontoxic and impermeable, and it could "deadfold"—lock in place around food or containers without tape or other fasteners.

By the 1970s, aluminum foil was a staple in almost every U.S. kitchen, so it's no surprise that Scouts and campers began using it for outdoor cooking. It provided a simple way to put together a meal with little cleanup required afterward.

Over the years, foil packets have delighted each new generation as veterans showed young people how to cook in foil.

The explosion of the internet has made it somewhat easier to pass along information, and foil-wrapped meal packs have become more diverse. Most middle-aged adults fondly recall their hamburger camp packs, while kids today may have salmon or cauliflower packs to satisfy alternate food tastes and needs.

Scouts and campers continue to pass along the tradition of foil-packet cooking outdoors, but now families make oven foil packs at home, too. People who live alone can enjoy the simplicity of making a single meal in foil, and older adults may appreciate premade, heat-and-eat foil packs that involve virtually no cleanup. Aluminum foil packets are super simple to make and can include unlimited combinations of meat and vegetables, with flavors nicely layered by the contained cooking. Even if you only have leftovers in your refrigerator, you have the makings of a delicious packet meal. Your imagination is the only limit.

TOOLS FOR FOIL-PACKET GRILLING

As with any craft, cooking with aluminum foil is much easier, and success rates are higher when you use the right tools. A plus for both those who love to grill in foil packets and those just testing the waters is that the investment price is quite low. Most accessories are readily available at big-box stores or online. Many can be found at resale or consignment shops, too.

Turner: A jumbo turner is super helpful for making aluminum foil packs. While you can use a standard kitchen turner, it won't span the width of the pack and you'll likely end up with tears in the foil.

Tongs: Tongs are handy if you are cooking over flames. Tongs give you more reach and keep your hand and body back from the direct heat as you put food on to cook, remove, flip, turn, or readjust meal packs.

Avoid tongs with jagged edges, which could tear the foil when you grab the pack. If the foil tears, the steam is released and you won't have even cooking.

Mandoline: When putting together foil packs, it's important to have thin slices of uniform thickness. You can produce even slices with a mandoline, and it's much faster than using a knife. Mandolines are especially nice for slicing classic foil-packet ingredients such as potatoes and onions. Do note that they may not work as well for really hard root vegetables such as winter squash, or for soft foods such as most tomatoes.

Grill Gloves: Gloves made for grilling or smoking work really well for foil-packet grilling. They protect your hands from the heat and allow you to turn or remove packs from the grate or coals without using metal utensils that could puncture the foil.

REGULATING HEAT LEVELS

Regulation of heat is important when grilling in foil. Since you can't see through the foil, you need to have a general idea of how long the food needs to be over or surrounded by the flame. In most cases you'll want a medium heat for foil cooking, around 350°F.

Judging heat levels is more art than science, even if you have a built-in grill thermometer. One fairly reliable test is to put your hand about six inches above the flames or coals. If you pull your hand back around the six-second mark, then the coals are in the medium range. Pulling back within four seconds or less is hot while being able to hold for eight seconds or more suggests low heat.

Gas Grills: Many gas grills have knobs to adjust the heat from low to high, but on most grills the heat is rather inconsistent. If you want high heat, then turning the burners up to high and leaving the lid open and foil packets over the flames generally work fine. The best way to get medium heat is to have half the burners or elements turned on and half turned off. With the lid down on a gas grill and the food placed on the side without the flames, the grill becomes a rather efficient outdoor cooker for making perfectly grilled foil packets. Add approximately five minutes per twenty minutes of grill time if the grill lid is open and times need to be fairly exact. Low heat is also most easily achieved with an offset and closed lid, but it's usually fine to run the knob at low heat and to let the foil packs grill over modest heat. Most foil packets that are placed over low heat is for warming up the food rather than cooking it.

Charcoal Grills: It can be difficult to regulate charcoal. The key is to make sure the charcoal has burned down to coals rather than being at full flame (except in rare instances). This is best achieved by using a chimney starter, which takes about fifteen minutes to get coals red and layered with white ash to be prepared for grilling. A chimney starter full of charcoal works for almost all foil-packet cook times, but you can add coals by lighting another chimney starter full of coals as needed and putting them on the grill. It is also helpful to have the coals all on one side of the grill in an offset. When the foil packs are set on the cooler side and the lid is placed on the grill, the temperature tends to be consistently medium as the heat circulates. If you need high heat, don't offset the coals. For low heat, use the offset method and put the food packs to the cool side, but don't put the lid down on the grill.

Wood Fires: Campfire cooking can be the trickiest but also the most fun and memorable. When cooking over wood, be sure to burn the fuel down to red coals first. Foil packs can be placed on grates over the coals or set to the edge of them. It's especially important to flip and/or rotate your foil packs when cooking over wood, since temperatures will vary more than with a gas or charcoal grill. The basic rule of thumb on campfire temperatures is that low heat is achieved when the foil packet is placed to the side of the coals, medium heat is achieved when the foil packet is placed over the coals to the outside edges, and high heat is achieved when the foil packet is directly over the hot coals.

Quick Tip: When in doubt about what temperature to use, try medium. It may not work as well as lower or higher heat in specific cases, but you're not likely to have a total disaster if you use moderate heat and make adjustments based on your own signature grilling style.

One thing that will help you hone your skills is taking notes. Keep track of the type and size of your heat source and how your recipes turn out. I find it easiest to do this right in whatever cookbook I'm using. That way I have a good starting point when I decide to make the same dish again. Though I may be sure that I'll remember the details later, often that's just not the case.

FOODS FOR FOIL

Many foods can be grilled in foil packs, which are really like miniature ovens or steam baths. Meats, vegetables, and some fruits do well, and they can be combined in numerous ways.

It's important to combine foods that require approximately the same amount of cooking time, though some variation works if you slice the slower-cooking items thinner. For example, most cuts of meat will cook more quickly than potato chunks, so slicing the potatoes (especially using a mandoline) works better for foil grilling. Layers tend to work best in general, since they allow for better circulation.

Some food combinations simply do not work well in foil. Just because you see something online or in a cookbook doesn't necessarily mean that it's going to work out. For example, I see a lot of recipes calling for corn on the cob together with shrimp. But shrimp cooks really fast. Drop shrimp in boiling water, and it's done in two or three minutes. Compare that to corn, which I generally boil for fifteen to twenty-five minutes. If those foods are combined in the same foil pack, then either the corn will be crunchy or the shrimp will be rubbery. Both can be cooked in foil, just not in the same pack if you want good results.

There are ways to get around some variations in grilling times. If you have an item that will cook faster than the other ingredients, place it at the top of the foil pack. Rotate the pack instead of flipping it, so the faster-cooking food gets less intense heat. This works well if you want to combine a fast-cooking vegetable such as squash with chicken or pork. Just put the squash at the top of the pack, and it will be fine.

If you love to bake, you really need to stay in the kitchen. While it is possible to bake bread, cakes, cookies, and even pies outdoors, it takes a lot of time, skill, and oftentimes just plain luck to get good results. I'd rather invest my efforts in foods that are better suited to cooking outdoors and in foil packs.

SEASONINGS

Play around with different seasonings for your foil pack cooking. One of the great things about making little food packs is that the flavors are quite intense because of the consolidated cooking area. If you've only been using salt and pepper (which are great, of course), you are missing out on tons of delicious flavors that can turn a "meh" foil package into a real winner. If you don't have a good source of herbs and seasonings in your area, you can find a slew of flavors online. I find some of my favorites on Amazon and Penzeys online.

Here are some of the favorite seasonings around my home:

Pepper: Yes, you have pepper at home, but it's likely standard ground black pepper. Using your own grinder and peppercorns, the flavor will be fresher and more intense.

You can also introduce all kinds of interesting flavors, from sweet to intensely hot, by using different pepper seeds and ground peppers. Go easy with any new pepper—especially in foil packs, which amplify flavors. You can always add more after a dish is cooked if you need additional pop.

Salt: When I was a kid, salt was salt. You bought a blue container of salt and filled up your shaker. Today, however, a variety of salts are available. If you've not tried kosher, sea, Himalayan, pink, or smoked salt, you may be surprised that salt can come in various flavors. A meal can also be dressed up or down with different grinds, from very fine to coarse. I especially like finely ground sea salt and pink salt in a coarse grind.

Garlic: You'll find garlic packaged and sold in a variety of ways, from fresh garlic in the produce section to garlic salts, sprinkles, and bottled minced garlic. I do prefer fresh garlic, and it is easy to use. Just peel off the papery outer layers and inside you'll find several individual garlic cloves; place a clove under the blade of a kitchen knife and quickly but firmly press to use whole in recipes, or chop or mince. If you prefer not to work with fresh garlic or you need something to keep in the cabinet for last-minute seasoning, some processed versions are quite tasty, too.

Lemon Pepper: My college roommate introduced me to lemon pepper, and it was love at first taste. This flexible mix is now a staple at my house. It is great for perking up meat or vegetables. In fact, there are few dishes that don't work with lemon pepper. If you are stumped for seasonings for a foil dish, just sprinkle on some lemon pepper for a mild but pleasing flavor addition.

Italian Dressing: One of my outdoor kitchen secrets is bottled oil-based Italian dressing, especially the spicy version. Just shake on a few spoonfuls to add a burst of flavor, or use Italian dressing as a marinade. It not only gives flavor to meat or vegetables, it also helps tenderize your meat.

Seasoning Blends: Don't be afraid to try commercial seasoning blends. Someone took the time to combine various flavors in various ratios to come up with a tasty product. You won't love all blends, but most of them are quite good or they wouldn't have made it out of the test kitchens. If you find one that you love, try other blends from the same manufacturer.

HOW TO FOLD YOUR FOIL PACK

There are several ways to fold food in foil packs. Some work better than others, depending on what's in the pack, but it's generally a matter of preference. In most cases, what's important is getting a good crimp and seal. Foil packs generally cook by means of a buildup of steam inside, so loose or gappy folding can mean uneven cooking, or even burning.

Basic Blanket Fold: The most common fold for foil packs is the blanket fold, which involves placing food on a piece of foil, topping it with a second piece the same size, and then crimping (folding the edges together into tight, small sections or ridges) the four sides closed.

Tented Blanket Fold: Think of the tented blanket fold as a variation of the basic blanket fold. The only difference is that the top layer of aluminum foil is slightly larger than the bottom piece for this version. When crimping the edges, fluff up the top layer of foil so there is some extra air space inside. This works especially well for meal packs that might otherwise stick to the foil at the top.

One-Sheet Fold: Pull off a piece of foil approximately twice as long as you'd use for a blanket fold. Then fold in half so the cut ends meet and crimp together the longer side and one of the two shorter sides so that it resembles a sleeping bag. Slide the food into the remaining opening and crimp to seal. This works well when foods are mixed together before grilling. It's also a good method for kids to use because the food is less likely to fall out.

One-Sheet Tented Fold: Pull two sides together at the top like a tent with the food in the bottom. Fold down and press tight, leaving space. Roll the two ends up and press tight to seal. You should have a pack that looks a bit like a pocketbook and is sealed at the top on both ends.

Aluminum Foil Crunch: In a few cases the food simply needs to be protected from the heat, and capturing steam isn't important—for baked potatoes and apples, for instance. The foil crunch is just what it sounds like: you simply mash aluminum foil around the food to completely cover it.

Pan Top Cover Crunch: Some dishes are difficult to make in traditional foil packs. They may be extra-large or kind of floppy, or they may have toppings such as cheese that can easily stick to the top of basic foil packages. A good way to expand your options is to use a disposable foil pan and then seal a sheet of aluminum foil over the top.

And when grilling for a family, this method takes less grill space than individual foil packs would.

HOW TO KEEP FOOD FROM SCORCHING OR BURNING

Everyone tends to be more forgiving when food is cooked outside. That's good, because it's hard to achieve perfect results. A fire will have different levels of heat. The outdoor ambient temperature will have an impact. Your timing may be off, or you may be distracted by all the activity that typically surrounds an outdoor cooking space. To increase your odds of having a masterpiece (or even a "good enough" meal), here are a few little hacks that will stack the deck in your favor.

Turning/Rotating: An obvious way to avoid uneven grilling is to flip or rotate your foil packs. Since lid-on grilling is faster and more even as far as temperatures go, do not go wild with the flipping and rotating. For most recipes you will only want to reposition the packet about every ten minutes.

Ice Cubes: You can use ice cubes to keep the heat from rising too quickly inside your foil pack and also to provide extra moisture. Just add two or three ice cubes or a handful of ice chips to each foil pack and increase the grilling time slightly.

Cabbage Leaf: A fun way to prevent sticking or burning in foil is to sandwich your foods between cabbage leaves. Simply place a cabbage leaf on the foil, arrange your food on top of it, cover with another cabbage leaf, and add the top layer of foil.

Bacon Layer: Lining the bottom of your foil pack with bacon provides a barrier that greatly reduces the chance of burning. The bacon also adds flavor, of course, so you probably don't want to use it with a dessert pack. But most other recipes work fine with bacon on the bottom of the packet.

Onion Bed: Placing thick slices of onion on the bottom of your foil pack makes the main ingredients less likely to scorch. The onion takes the heat and ends up with the char, if there is any. Some people love onion that's grilled to a crisp, so you'll likely have a few guests who enjoy the burnt onions almost as much as the protected main meal.

TYPES OF ALUMINUM FOIL

You can't make foil packets without aluminum foil, and buying foil seems pretty basic. Then you get to the store, and there are OPTIONS. While all foil rolls can be used for outdoor grilling, some types do work better for some foil packs. You can use whatever aluminum foil you have on hand, but if you are purchasing foil for outdoor cooking, you may want to consider the benefits of the different types.

Standard Foil: The gauge on standard aluminum foil is typically .63 mil. You may want to double the sheets, especially if the pack will be in direct contact with wood or charcoal.

Heavy-Duty Foil: Most heavy-duty foil in the United States is rolled to a thickness of .94 mil. That extra aluminum means that your foil packages are less likely to break or tear when you handle them.

Nonstick Aluminum Foil: Nonstick foil looks like standard aluminum foil, but the dull side is a little more textured. You'll want to be sure that the dull side is what's in contact with the food, since you are paying for the extra benefit of nonstick grilling.

Grilling Foil: The latest version of aluminum foil is grilling foil that combines heavy-duty and nonstick properties.

Aluminum Foil Trays/Pans: Foil trays or pans can expand your options. You use the pan in place of the bottom layer of foil and then cover with a sheet of foil over the top. This gives you the same effect as traditional foil-packet cooking, but the sturdier base lets you make floppier dishes and larger quantities. You can also achieve better results with sticky ingredients like barbecue sauce or cheese, since the sides of the pan can lift the foil top up and away from them. Just place easier-to-burn items on top when loading up your foil pan.

A good rule of thumb is to plan for 1¼ to ½ inch of air space at the top of the pan once it is loaded with food.

Quick Tip: Sometimes one type of foil does work better than others for a particular meal pack. For example, high heat and thinner foil may be used to give food some crispiness. Nonstick foil may be needed or preferred to keep an ingredient from sticking. After you have some experience grilling with aluminum foil, you will begin to anticipate which types work best in which situations.

Shiny or Dull Side?

Arguments about the benefits of folding the shiny side of aluminum to the inside or outside of a cooking pack are as classic as camp snipe-hunt stories. While it's fun to listen to someone wax eloquent about the question of foil reflectivity, there's no science to back up claims of foil finish properties related to outdoor cooking benefits.

In the factory, aluminum foil is fed through rollers two sheets at a time due to its thinness. The aluminum that comes in contact with the rollers is shiny, while the sides that are sandwiched to the inside, aluminum to aluminum, are dull. It's simply a production oddity. It really makes no difference which side is folded in or out when you are cooking, although it can be fun to have a philosophical discussion about it.

RECYCLING ALUMINUM FOIL

The average American throws away three pounds of aluminum foil every year. Since aluminum foil is 100% recyclable, it seems like a no-brainer that it should be sent to the recycling center.

Unfortunately, however, many recycling centers don't accept aluminum foil. The key reason is that it's not cost effective. Compared to aluminum cans, the weight of aluminum foil is much less after cleaning—and foil is generally much dirtier. If you've used aluminum foil on a Thanksgiving turkey or in foil packs with cheese, you'll understand the issue. Also, aluminum foil is thin and hard to process automatically. Small scraps or little balls of foil can stop up equipment. When lines come to a halt, nothing is getting recycled.

You can check online at https://recyclenation.com to see if aluminum foil is recycled in your area. It is ideal if it can be put back into the system, since clean aluminum foil is 100% recyclable.

If you can't recycle your aluminum foil, reuse it at home. Foil can be cleaned. Just hand-wash or put on the top rack of your dishwasher with the food-crusted side down and glasses or other heavy items on top to hold it in place. Washed foil can be used in many ways. One of my favorites is to mash it into a loose ball and use it as a cheap and effective way to clean the grill grates. Just preheat the grill a bit and wipe away. Unfortunately, the foil cannot be reused for new foil packets. The packs get very messy. Washing the foil could result in tiny tears, which would not hold in the steam as required.

Quick Tip: If you have questions about where to recycle specific things, visit Earth911 at https://search.earth911.com. Select the items you want to recycle from the extensive database and plug in your zip code to find the locations closest to you in North America. Or you can call 1-800-CLEANUP.

MAIN MEALS

Classic Hobo Pack

A hobo pack is typically one of the first camping meals a child makes independently, and the memories of assembling a campfire feast last forever. Variations on the traditional hobo pack are virtually endless, but the base generally consists of sliced potatoes and a thin hamburger patty. Seasonings and firm vegetables round out and give personality to individual foil packs. It's almost impossible to ruin hobo packs, so they are a great way to spark a lifelong interest in cooking.

MAKES: 1 serving | **PREP TIME:** 10 minutes | **GRILL TIME:** 30 to 45 minutes |
REST TIME: 5 minutes

Foil needed: 2 (12 x 12-inch) pieces

1 baseball-size potato, sliced in 1¼ -inch-thick rounds

2 slices yellow onion

1¼ pounds ground beef, formed into a ½-inch-thick patty

1 teaspoon Lawry's Seasoned Salt

1 teaspoon lemon pepper

1¼ cups zesty, oil-based Italian dressing

1 tablespoon dried parsley flakes

salt and pepper, to taste

1. Arrange the potato and onion slices in the center of the first foil sheet.

2. Place the hamburger patty on top of the potato/onion layer.

3. Sprinkle the meat with the seasoning salt and lemon pepper, then pour the Italian dressing on top.

4. Sprinkle the parsley over the potatoes and meat patty.

5. Top with the second piece of foil and seal all edges tightly, leaving room in the top of the pack to allow steam to build up.

6. Grill over medium heat for 30 to 45 minutes.

7. Remove the foil pack from the heat. Let rest for 5 minutes before opening, then sprinkle with salt and pepper to taste.

Fun Fact: Hobos were men (and a few women) who were a cross between migrant workers and the homeless. During the Great Depression, hobos often hitched rides (illegally) on railroad cars. Most took jobs when they could find them, although work could be spotty and hard to secure. People like to imagine that hobos wrapped food in foil and placed it over fire for occasional hot meals, and the idea isn't that farfetched.

Soup-er Hobo Pack

There are endless variations of the classic hobo foil packet, and one of the favorites is this version using cream of mushroom soup. The soup itself already includes seasonings, so you don't really need to add anything other than salt and pepper (and remember that canned soup already contains a lot of salt).

MAKES: 1 serving | **PREP TIME:** 10 minutes | **GRILL TIME:** 40 minutes | **REST TIME:** 5 minutes

Foil needed: 2 (12 x 12-inch) pieces

½ (10½-ounce) can condensed cream of mushroom soup

1/3 pound lean ground beef, formed into a patty

1 medium potato, cut in bite-size chunks

1 small onion, diced

salt and pepper, to taste

1. Spray a foil sheet with nonstick cooking spray.

2. Spoon about half of the can of soup into the center of the foil.

3. Place the ground beef patty on top of the soup.

4. Add the potato and onion on top of the beef patty, then pour the remaining can of soup over the top.

5. Seal the foil with a second sheet of foil, leaving some space at the top.

6. Grill over medium heat for 40 minutes.

7. Let rest for 5 minutes before opening, then season with salt and pepper to taste.

Fun Fact: If you ask your grandparents or even your great-grandparents about condensed soups, they will likely remember them as mealtime staples—a bowl of soup with salty soda crackers. A can of water or milk was added as the soup was heated to make a warm lunch or dinner. For a hobo meal, you don't need to add liquid—the meal creates its own steam. If you find that your soup-er hobo meals are turning out a bit too thick, add an ice cube before sealing the pack.

Beef Cubes

There are times when I like to showcase a single ingredient. That's the case with these beef cubes. While beef can be used all sorts of ways, with loads of other ingredients, it is a wonderful stand-alone ingredient. When you have a craving for beef, you can't miss with this delicious dish. This dish can also be paired with grilled baked potatoes or foil pack summer vegetables.

MAKES: 4 small servings | **PREP TIME:** 20 minutes | **GRILL TIME:** 30 minutes | **REST TIME:** 5 minutes
Foil needed: 8 (12 x 12-inch) pieces

MARINADE INGREDIENTS:

¼ cup balsamic vinegar

2 tablespoons olive oil

2 tablespoons low sodium soy sauce

1 tablespoon Worcestershire sauce

BEEF CUBE INGREDIENTS:

1 pound top sirloin steak

6 tablespoons (¾ stick) butter

2 teaspoons minced garlic

kosher salt and freshly ground pepper, to taste

1 tablespoon chopped fresh parsley

1. In a medium bowl, combine the marinade ingredients.

2. Cut the steak in 1½-inch chunks, removing any excess fat and gristle, and pour the marinade mix over the meat. It's best if you can do this an hour before putting foil packs together.

3. Melt the butter in a small pan over low heat on the stovetop or grill.

4. Stir in the garlic, salt, and pepper.

5. Set out 4 pieces of foil and place beef chunks in the center of each.

6. Drizzle butter over the beef chunks for each.

7. Cover each piece with the remaining foil and seal on all sides, using a blanket fold.

8. Grill each foil packet over medium-high heat for 15 minutes. Then, flip and grill for another 15 minutes.

9. Carefully puncture the top layer of each packet to allow steam to release after removing from the grill, and let rest for 5 minutes.

10. For added visual appeal, put all servings of beef chunks on the hot grill grates for 30 seconds, then flip and grill for an additional 30 seconds, or until the beef is caramelized and has grill marks.

11. Garnish with the parsley just before serving each packet.

Fun Fact: Are grill marks critical for making your grilled meat tasty? The answer to that question is "no"—branding food with crosshatch marks is simply showmanship. Most people don't notice a flavor difference. We do eat with our eyes as well as our taste buds, though, so if you want to mark or brown up food, it's all good. Grill-marked food does have great eye appeal.

Using high heat to brown meat with the Maillard reaction—a chemical interaction between amino acids and sugars—does change the molecular structure of food and adds flavor. But that is best achieved with even browning across the entire surface of the food. And yes, you can do that on hot grill grates.

Quick Tip: You can purchase grill grates when caramelizing the beef chunks to avoid your food falling between the grates.

Steak Teriyaki with Vegetables

The most common type of restaurant in the United States is Asian. Even my very tiny town of 832 people has a small Chinese buffet restaurant along with fried chicken sold at the gas station. While I enjoy having Asian food always available, I also like to make my own Asian-inspired foil packs from scratch.

MAKES: 4 servings | **PREP TIME:** 15 minutes | **GRILL TIME:** 25 minutes | **REST TIME:** 10 minutes

Foil needed: 8 (12 x 12-inch) pieces

½ pound steak (such as rib-eye, T-bone, or filet mignon), cut in 1½ by ½-inch chunks

½ cup teriyaki marinade

4 red-skinned baby potatoes, cut in 1-inch chunks with skin left on

1 cup broccoli florets

1 small purple onion, cut in bite-size pieces

1 small green bell pepper, cut in bite-size pieces

salt and pepper, to taste

1. Combine the steak chunks and teriyaki marinade in a medium bowl.

2. Add the potatoes, broccoli, onion, and bell pepper. Stir until all the ingredients are evenly coated with the marinade.

3. Divide the ingredients equally among 4 foil pieces. Season with salt and pepper.

4. Top each portion with another foil piece; seal the edges to complete blanket-style packets.

5. Grill for 15 minutes over medium-high heat. Then flip the packet over and grill for an additional 10 minutes.

6. Remove the packets from the grill and let rest for 10 minutes to allow all the vegetables to finish cooking.

Quick Tip: You can buy teriyaki marinade, but it's easy to make your own. In a quart jar, combine 1 cup soy sauce, 1 cup water, 1/3 cup brown sugar, 1¼ cups olive oil, and 1 tablespoon Worcestershire sauce. Add ground ginger, onion powder, and garlic powder to taste. I start with ½ teaspoon each and adjust if needed. Fasten on the jar lid and shake to blend.

Barbecued Pork Chop

This is one of the easiest foil packets that I make. All I have to do is add barbecue sauce to a pork chop and cook it in foil on the grill. The barbecue sauce is what makes it interesting.

I've tried hundreds of barbecue sauces over the years, and there are loads more still to try. People are constantly bottling their favorite family barbecue sauces and putting them on the market. I enjoy making this main dish with new sauces and also with old favorites.

MAKES: 1 serving | **PREP TIME:** 5 minutes | **GRILL TIME:** 20 minutes | **REST TIME:** 5 minutes
Foil needed: 1 (12 x 12-inch) piece

1 boneless pork chop (approximately ½ inch thick)

½ cup favorite barbecue sauce

1. Lightly spray the aluminum foil with nonstick cooking spray.

2. Place the pork chop in the center of the foil, then pour the barbecue sauce over the chop.

3. Bring the aluminum foil up and over the pork chop, folding to make a tent-like package with air space at the top to prevent the barbecue sauce from burning.

4. Grill over medium heat for 20 minutes.

5. Allow the pack to rest for 5 minutes before opening.

Fun Fact: The most common type of barbecue sauce sold in grocery stores is tomato based. Other styles are mostly associated with the southern United States. In the Piedmont and beach areas of North Carolina, vinegar-based sauce is popular. South Carolina is known for mustard-based sauce. And Alabama checks in with barbecue sauce made from mayonnaise. If you start looking globally, the options are virtually endless.

Pork Chop with Mushroom Gravy

Gravy turns any foil pack into comfort food. I always think of my grandma when I make this recipe, but I don't have to make a roux with flour and time perfectly. That makes this one a real winner and easy for anyone to make and enjoy.

MAKES: 1 serving | **PREP TIME:** 15 minutes | **GRILL TIME:** 25 minutes | **REST TIME:** 5 minutes

Foil needed: 2 (12 x 12-inch) pieces

1 medium potato, sliced in 1/16-inch-thick circles

1 boneless pork chop

1/2 can condensed cream of mushroom soup

1 ice cube

pepper, to taste

1. Spray a piece of aluminum foil with nonstick cooking spray.

2. Place the potatoes in the center of the foil and position the pork chop on top of the potatoes.

3. Spoon the soup over the pork chop.

4. Set the ice cube on top of the soup-covered pork chop and season with pepper.

5. Bring the foil ends together over the pork chop and seal, then seal the sides.

6. Grill over medium heat for 25 minutes.

7. Remove from the heat and let rest for 5 minutes. The steam coming from this pack will be very hot, so be careful as you open it.

Quick Tip: Canned soup makes a quick, easy, and tasty gravy in foil packs. Although it is customary to mix condensed soup with water in a 50:50 ratio, that makes the gravy too thin. I've found that a single ice cube adds just enough moisture, and it also increases the steam in the pack.

Ham Steak

Ham with pineapple, a cherry, and brown sugar always reminds me of my grandmother. She liked to make "fancy ham" for Sunday dinner, the midday meal right after church. Everyone in the family and sometimes friends came for Sunday dinner.

I don't have a big family living close by now, so a whole ham would go begging. To get that nostalgic feeling from days gone by, I just use a ham steak and the toppings that I remember from my childhood. With ham steaks, I can make a main dish to serve one or as many people as I want.

MAKES: 1 serving | **PREP TIME:** 5 minutes | **GRILL TIME:** 15 minutes | **REST TIME:** 5 minutes

Foil needed: 2 (12 x 12-inch) pieces

1 fully cooked ham steak, about ½ inch thick

1 canned pineapple slice

1 maraschino cherry

1 tablespoon brown sugar

1 tablespoon orange juice

1. Place the ham steak in the center of a foil piece.

2. Top the ham with the pineapple slice, then add the maraschino cherry in the center hole.

3. Sprinkle the brown sugar over the ham and pineapple. Drizzle on the orange juice.

4. Place the second sheet of foil over the top and seal on all sides.

5. Grill over medium heat for 15 minutes. Let rest 5 minutes before opening the pack.

Fun Fact: You may be wondering: "What is a ham steak?" Well, it's just a slice cut from a ham, next to the bone but not including any bone. Sizes and thicknesses can vary quite a bit. You can cut your own ham steaks from a whole cooked ham or buy them already cut.

Hawaiian Pork Chop

When my boys were little, I saved the top from a pineapple to try growing one at home. Yes, it does work! When my grandfather visited, he asked about our unusual houseplant. I said we were growing a pineapple, and he laughed and said it would never work—because pineapples grow underground! I have no idea where he got that idea, but I couldn't convince him that pineapples grow above ground on a stalk. Unfortunately, he wasn't around to see our pineapple plant develop right in our living room.

We get a laugh, remembering this little misunderstanding, when we make these Hawaiian pork chops in foil.

MAKES: 1 serving | **PREP TIME:** 15 minutes | **GRILL TIME:** 20 minutes | **REST TIME:** 5 minutes

Foil needed: 2 (12 x 9-inch) pieces

1 boneless pork chop

1 tablespoon pineapple chunks, plus 1 tablespoon of the pineapple juice

1 tablespoon diced green pepper

1 tablespoon diced onion

salt and pepper, to taste

1. Lightly spray a foil piece with nonstick cooking spray.

2. Place the pork chop in the center of the piece of foil.

3. Arrange the pineapple chunks, green pepper, and onion on top of the pork chop; drizzle on the pineapple juice.

4. Top with the second piece of foil and seal shut on all sides.

5. Grill for 20 minutes over medium heat.

6. Let rest for 5 minutes, then open and season to taste with salt and pepper.

Fun Fact: Most Americans think of Hawaii when they think of pineapples, but the world's top pineapple-producing area is Costa Rica. Some 90% of all pineapples consumed in the United States come from Costa Rica, and two out of three pineapples traded globally originate there. That's a lot of pineapples, considering that the demand for the fruit has grown 300% since 2000, as mentioned in "Costa Rica's Pineapple Industry: Sweet or Sour?". People love pineapples—they are inexpensive, travel well, and have a good shelf life. Oh, yes—they also taste delicious!

Meaty Mixed Beans

I live in North Carolina barbecue country, which means that I live close to a lot of restaurants that sell chopped pork. It also means that I have ready access to pork butts and shoulders, and I enjoy smoking them on our own smoker. I love our local meat, but smoking a shoulder or even a butt makes a whole lot of food. After a couple or three days, we get tired of pork sandwiches, however fabulous they may be. My solution is to use some of the meat to make these meaty beans. The first time I made it, I wasn't sure how much we'd like this dish, but it has turned out to be a favorite. Now we can enjoy our pork for a holiday meal and then look forward to having the leftovers in this yummy bean dish.

MAKES: 6 servings | **PREP TIME:** 10 minutes | **GRILL TIME:** 25 minutes | **REST TIME:** serve immediately

Foil needed: 1 (12 x 9-inch) pan and 1 (12 x 12-inch) piece

1 (15-ounce) can white beans, drained

1 (15-ounce) can red kidney beans, drained

1 (15-ounce) can black beans, drained

1 (14-ounce) can pork and beans, undrained

1 (14.5-ounce) can petite diced tomatoes, undrained

1 small white onion, finely diced

1¼ cups honey

2 teaspoons hot sauce

2 cups cooked pulled or chopped pork meat chips, for serving

1. In a large bowl, mix together all the beans; stir well.

2. Stir in the tomatoes, onion, honey, and hot sauce.

3. Fold in the pork.

4. Pour the mixture into the aluminum foil pan. Cover with the foil piece and seal the edges.

5. Grill for 20 minutes over medium heat, stirring occasionally.

6. Remove the foil from the top and grill for an additional 5 minutes, until the mixture is as thick as desired.

7. Spoon into bowls to serve, passing chips to accompany the beans.

Chicken Salsa

It took a lot of food to fill up my boys when they were in middle and high school, so I came up with this hearty Tex-Mex recipe that became a family favorite. My younger son says it reminds him of lasagna but with potatoes instead of noodles. He also suggests that you can double or triple the amount of cheese if you want. He does like his food extra cheesy!

MAKES: 2 servings | **PREP TIME:** 20 minutes | **GRILL TIME:** 1 hour and 15 minutes | **REST TIME:** 5 minutes

Foil needed: 1 (9 x 9-inch) pan and 1 (12 x 15-inch) nonstick piece

olive oil

2 medium potatoes

½ pound boneless, skinless chicken strips or 2 thin-sliced (½-inch) chicken breast halves

2 tablespoons taco seasoning

1 tablespoon chopped fresh cilantro (optional)

1 (16-ounce) jar salsa

8 ounces shredded Mexican cheese blend

1. Use a paper towel to distribute olive oil evenly over the bottom of the foil pan.

2. Slice the potatoes in $\frac{1}{16}$-inch slices; a mandoline works best for this. Arrange the potato slices in the bottom of the pan so they come about halfway up the sides.

3. Top the potatoes with the chicken pieces, then sprinkle on the taco seasoning and the cilantro, if using.

4. Pour on the salsa and spread it evenly over the meal. Top with the shredded cheese.

5. Tent the foil sheet over the pan, leaving some space above the cheese to prevent sticking. Seal the foil to the pan edges.

6. Grill over low heat, grill lid closed, for 1 hour and 15 minutes. Let rest 5 minutes before opening and serving.

Quick Tip: You can change up any dish that features salsa by using different types—switching from red to green salsa for a flavor shift, for example. Or select a salsa that contains beans, corn, or fruit for a completely new spin on a family favorite.

Fajitas in Foil Pan

Fajitas are fun to make and can be customized easily. Prepare the basic mix and then let everyone put together his or her own grill pack. Set up a topping station with favorites such as guacamole, sour cream, pica de gallo, salsa, and jalapeños. Be sure to have plenty of cheese, too. This meal is hard to beat for ease of preparation, flavor, and fun.

MAKES: 4 servings | **PREP TIME:** 10 minutes | **GRILL TIME:** 15 minutes | **REST TIME:** 5 minutes

Foil needed: 8 (12 x 9-inch) pieces

1 pound boneless, skinless chicken breast, cut in bite-size pieces

2 medium green bell peppers, cut in thin strips

1 small purple onion, sliced crosswise and separated into rings

3 tablespoons fajita seasoning

1¼ cups olive oil

8-inch flour tortillas

shredded cheese of choice

fajita toppings, such as guacamole, sour cream, pico de gallo, salsa, sliced jalapeños

1. Place the chicken, pepper strips, onion rings, fajita seasoning, and olive oil in a gallon-size zip-top plastic bag. Seal the bag and massage with your fingers to distribute the oil and seasonings evenly over the chicken and vegetables.

2. Divide the mixture into 4 equal portions and place on the foil pieces.

3. Add the top layer of foil over each portion and crimp the edges shut.

4. Grill over medium-high heat, grill lid closed, for 15 minutes, flipping over once.

5. Let rest for 5 minutes, then open and serve with two tortillas per pack, and add toppings as desired.

Quick Tip: Have your diners assemble their own individual foil packets and write their names on the foil with a Sharpie pen. Everyone enjoys arranging their own packet, and then it's fun to compare the results.

Chunky Chicken Chili

Chili is one of my favorite camp meals. It's really a one-pot meal, or in this case a one-pack meal. The flavors of the meat and vegetables along with the kick of heat create the ultimate in comfort food for me. And while I love a good beef chili, I especially like this full-bodied and not-too-soupy chicken version—especially nice if you are eating your chili right out of the foil.

MAKES: 1 serving | **PREP TIME:** 5 minutes | **GRILL TIME:** 15 minutes | **REST TIME:** 10 minutes

Foil needed: 2 (12 x 12-inch) pieces

½ cup canned Rotel tomatoes

1 cup canned white beans, rinsed and drained

½ cup canned corn, rinsed and drained

1 cup shredded cooked chicken (grocery store rotisserie chicken is great for this)

½ cup shredded cheddar cheese

1 single-serving bag of corn chips, such as Fritos

1. Combine the tomatoes, beans, corn, and chicken in a medium bowl, mixing well.

2. Lightly spray a piece of foil with nonstick cooking spray.

3. Spoon the mixture onto the foil.

4. Top with the second piece of foil and seal the edges tightly.

5. Grill for 15 minutes over medium-high heat.

6. Let stand for 10 minutes, then open and top with cheese and corn chips.

Quick Tip: I've found that kids love chili-chip bags. Carefully open a single serving bag of corn chips and spoon in as much chili as will fit without spilling over. Pass out your chili bags and spoons, and everyone can happily walk around with a truly portable meal.

Low-Country Foil Boil

You will feel like you've landed on the East Coast of the United States when you try this recipe. Although low-country boil is traditionally made in a pot of boiling water, foil packets give you almost the same result but in smaller batches and requiring less equipment.

I do suggest using only sausage for the meat in this dish, although you'll see shrimp as a key ingredient along the coast. The issue with shrimp is that it cooks really quickly, so it is added when a traditional boil is almost done. With foil packs, everything cooks for the same amount of time, so the shrimp gets rubbery before the other foods are cooked through.

MAKES: 1 serving | **PREP TIME:** 20 minutes | **GRILL TIME:** 25 minutes | **REST TIME:** 10 minutes

Foil needed: 1 (12 x 18-inch) piece

1 andouille chicken sausage, cut in ¾-inch slices (approximately 1/5 pound)

1 ear of corn, cut in 1-inch pieces

6 small red-skinned baby potatoes

2 teaspoons Old Bay seafood seasoning

4 ice cubes

Tabasco sauce, to taste

1 sliced lemon wedge (optional)

1. Place the sausage pieces, corn, and whole potatoes in the center of the foil sheet.

2. Sprinkle the seafood seasoning over the meat and vegetables.

3. Place the ice cubes on top of the food.

4. Fold the foil ends together over the meal and then seal the sides closed.

5. Grill over medium heat, grill lid closed, for 25 minutes.

6. Let rest for 10 minutes, then pour off the excess liquid and empty the contents of the pack onto several sheets of newspaper, which will absorb any extra water and eliminate the need for a plate (or even utensils).

7. Splash with Tabasco sauce and squeeze on lemon juice, as desired.

Fun Fact: This low-country boil is known as Frogmore Stew. No, there were never any frogs in the recipe; the dish originated in Frogmore, South Carolina, on the island of St. Helena near Beaufort. There are a lot of frogs along the southern coast, and they are very loud. But the coastal residents are not "eating" frogs.

Chicken and Stuffing

This foil packet main dish eats like a gourmet meal—perfect if you're camping or vacationing outdoors over a holiday. There's just something about stuffing that makes dinner seem extra special. And it is. But this is not a difficult dish to make—and you can celebrate anytime, after all, no matter what the calendar says.

MAKES: 4 servings | **PREP TIME:** 15 minutes | **GRILL TIME:** 30 minutes | **REST TIME:** 5 minutes

Foil needed: 8 (12 x 12-inch) heavy-duty pieces

1 (6-ounce) package chicken stuffing mix

1¼ cups water

1½ pounds boneless, skinless chicken tenders

4 cups bite-size broccoli pieces

4 slices bacon, fried and broken into bite-size pieces

1 cup shredded American or cheddar cheese

1¼ cups ranch dressing

1. Spray each piece of foil lightly with nonstick cooking spray.

2. In a medium bowl, mix together the stuffing mix and water.

3. Divide the stuffing into 4 portions and place on 4 foil sheets. Top each stuffing portion with a quarter of the chicken pieces.

4. Combine the broccoli, bacon, cheese, and ranch dressing in a large zip-top plastic bag. Massage the bag until the ingredients are evenly mixed, then divide the mixture into 4 portions and place on top of chicken.

5. Seal the foil packets with the four extra pieces of foil with air space at the top to prevent sticking or burning. Then grill over medium heat for 30 minutes, or until the chicken is done.

6. Vent with a knife to let out the excess steam, let rest for 5 minutes, and serve.

Fun Fact: Ranch is the most popular dressing in the United States. It started as a buttermilk-based dressing in Alaska. Afterward, the creator of the dressing moved to California and opened Hidden Valley Ranch with his wife, where it was modified as a packaged seasoning mix. The bottled version, which doesn't have to be refrigerated if still sealed, was rolled out in 1983. Bottled dressing is a godsend on camping trips.

Zippy Chicken Breast

This very basic chicken packet is delicious on its own but is also good served over foil-packet potatoes or rice made on a side burner or indoors on a stovetop. Other vegetables, such as zucchini or cabbage, can also be made in side packs to dress up the chicken.

MAKES: 1 serving | **PREP TIME:** 10 minutes | **GRILL TIME:** 35 minutes | **REST TIME:** 5 minutes

Foil needed: 1 (12 x 9-inch) piece

1 boneless, skinless chicken breast half

1 teaspoon lemon pepper

½ cup snapped green beans

½ cup broccoli florets

¼ cup zesty oil-based Italian dressing

1 slice lemon (optional)

1. Lightly spray the foil with nonstick cooking spray.

2. Place the chicken breast in the center of the foil and sprinkle with the lemon pepper.

3. Place green beans and broccoli on top of the chicken.

4. Pour the Italian dressing over the chicken.

5. Place a slice of lemon on top of the chicken and vegetables.

6. Pull the edges of the foil up and seal in a tent fold, with space above the food for steam to collect. Roll up the ends to complete the seal.

7. Grill over medium heat for 35 minutes.

8. Let rest for 5 minutes before serving.

Quick Tip: Oil-based Italian dressings can be used to marinate almost any meat, or as a flavor base that also prevents sticking to the foil. Unopened, these dressings do not need to be refrigerated, so Italian dressing makes a good staple for your outdoor cooking kitchen.

Chicken and Summer Vegetables

I really like this chicken foil packet recipe for its simplicity. It only involves stirring and cooking—no layers or anything complicated. It's also yummy, so it goes on our family rotation list.

MAKES: 4 servings | **PREP TIME:** 10 minutes | **GRILL TIME:** 20 minutes | **REST TIME:** 5 minutes

Foil needed: 8 (12 x 12-inch) pieces

4 boneless, skinless chicken breasts cut into bite-size pieces

4 small Roma tomatoes, sliced ½-inch thick

2 zucchini slices, sliced ½-inch thick

1 small onion, sliced crosswise and separated into rings

2 teaspoons minced garlic

2 tablespoons olive oil

1 teaspoon Aleppo pepper flakes

1 teaspoon smoked paprika

salt and pepper, to taste

1. Toss everything together in a medium bowl.

2. Divide the mixture into 4 portions and divide among the foil sheets.

3. Seal each foil pouch with a top layer of foil.

4. Grill for 20 minutes over medium-high heat.

5. Let rest for 5 minutes before serving.

Quick Tip: You can use various incarnations of garlic in recipes. As a rule of thumb, a clove of fresh garlic equals ½ teaspoon garlic salt, ½ teaspoon bottled minced garlic, 1¼ teaspoons granulated garlic, or ⅛ teaspoon garlic powder.

BBQ Chicken with Mango and Jalapeños

My family loves this quick and easy foil recipe featuring fresh mango. For different flavor notes, try various summer fruits as they come into season. Some of our favorites besides mango are cherry, pineapple, and peach.

MAKES: 1 serving | **PREP TIME:** 5 minutes | **GRILL TIME:** 20 minutes | **REST TIME:** 5 minutes

Foil needed: 2 (12 x 12-inch) pieces

1 boneless, skinless chicken breast half
½ cup barbecue sauce

1¼ cups cubed mango pieces
⅓ cup jalapeño slices

1. Spray a piece of foil with nonstick cooking spray.

2. Place the chicken breast in the center of the foil and pour the barbecue sauce over the chicken.

3. Arrange the mango pieces and jalapeño slices on top of the barbecue sauce.

4. Use the second foil sheet to close the packet, leaving extra breathing space so the barbecue sauce won't burn or stick.

5. Grill over medium heat for 20 minutes.

6. Let rest for 5 minutes before serving.

Quick Tip: A good way to get meats uniform in thickness for foil grilling is to use a meat mallet. Meat mallets are inexpensive to purchase, but if you don't have one, you can get a similar effect by putting your meat in a zip-top plastic bag and using a rolling pin.

Cheesy Flounder

This was a desperation dish. I hadn't been to the grocery store, so I had to make do with what was on hand. Pickings were pretty slim. I wasn't sure that the flavors would meld, but this dish hits the spot year after year—twenty years and counting.

MAKES: 2 servings | **PREP TIME:** 10 minutes | **GRILL TIME:** 40 minutes | **REST TIME:** 5 minutes

Foil needed: 1 (9 x 9-inch) pan and 1 (12 x 15-inch) piece

3 tablespoons butter

2 (4- to 6-ounce) flounder fillets

1 teaspoon lemon juice

2 slices purple onion, separated into rings

¼ cup finely shredded carrot

1 tablespoon chopped fresh parsley

salt and pepper, to taste

2 slices American or cheddar cheese

1. Melt the butter in the foil pan over a hot grill. Remove from the heat and gently shake to distribute the butter evenly across the pan bottom.

2. Carefully place the fish fillets in the melted butter.

3. Arrange the onion rings and shredded carrots on top of the fish.

4. Evenly sprinkle the parsley over the fish, season with salt and pepper, and top each fillet with a slice of cheese.

5. Place the foil sheet loosely over the top and seal tightly over the edges of the pan.

6. Grill over medium heat, grill lid closed, for 40 minutes, or until the fish is white inside and flakes easily.

7. Let rest for 5 minutes and then serve.

Quick Tip: Some foil pans are pretty pricey to use for single meals. I've found that dollar-type stores usually have the lowest prices, and Amazon has good deals for buying in bulk. Or you can have a dedicated metal pan for grilling and use a sheet of foil over the top to get the foil-packet effect—though you'll end up with fewer cleanup headaches if you use a disposable foil pan.

Mountain Trout Pack

My dad loved to fish more than anything else in the world. He would drop a pole on the first day of the fishing season and go as often as he could until the days began to cool. We enjoyed fresh trout on many a camping trip and at home. Yes, fresh fish can be cleaned and frozen for later. At home we usually had it fried (a Southern favorite), but this easy option was great when we were out in the pop-up camper. Fish in foil is one of the simplest main dishes you can make outdoors. (If you don't have access to fresh-caught mountain trout, substitute with pan-fried trout.)

MAKES: 1 serving (repeat for as many fish as you catch) | **PREP TIME:** 10 minutes | **GRILL TIME:** 25 minutes | **REST TIME:** 5 minutes

Foil needed: 1 (12 x 18-inch) piece

1 fresh-caught mountain trout, cleaned (approximately 10 to 12 inches long, or about 1 pound in weight), or pan-fried trout

1 tablespoon olive oil

3 thin slices lemon or lime

salt and pepper, to taste (sea salt and freshly ground pepper are really good)

1. Place the fish on the foil sheet and rub the olive oil over the outside and in the belly cavity.

2. Gently wedge the belly open far enough to insert the lemon or lime slices, and sprinkle on the seasonings.

3. Bring the edges of the foil piece up to tent the foil above the fish. Seal along the top and then seal the ends.

4. Grill over medium-high heat for 25 minutes, turning over twice.

5. Let rest for 5 minutes before opening the foil pack.

Quick Tip: Trout is done when the skin can be lifted away and the meat flakes easily from the bone. You can double-check for a temperature of 145°F in the thickest portion, but once you've seen trout cooked to the correct temperature, it's easy to tell if it has cooked enough by eyeballing it.

Grilled Wild Salmon

I didn't grow up eating salmon, because it wasn't readily available where I live. Fortunately, that has changed. Now salmon is available in most areas. That's great, because salmon is a very healthy fish to eat, loaded with omega-3 fatty acids and vitamin B12. I especially enjoy salmon when it is made quickly and easily in aluminum foil.

MAKES: 4 servings | **PREP TIME:** 5 minutes | **GRILL TIME:** 12 minutes | **REST TIME:** 5 minutes

Foil needed: 4 (12 x 9-inch) pieces

4 (6-ounce) salmon fillets, 1 inch thick, preferably wild-caught

1¼ cups olive oil

4 teaspoons Chef of the Future Cajun seasoning

freshly ground pepper, to taste

4 lemon slices

1. Spray the foil sheets very lightly with nonstick cooking spray.

2. Pat the salmon fillets with a paper towel to ensure that they are relatively dry. Rub the olive oil onto the salmon, using an equal amount for each fillet.

3. Sprinkle the Cajun seasoning and pepper onto the top and sides of each fillet.

4. Place a fillet on each sheet of foil and seal the edges shut.

5. Grill over medium heat, grill lid closed, for 12 minutes.

6. Squeeze one slice of lemon on each fillet, as desired.

7. Let rest for 5 minutes and then serve.

Fun Fact: Wild salmon typically has a pretty orange color due to its diet. In the wild, the healthy fish eat lots of shrimp and krill. Farm-raised salmon usually are given food with color additives to mimic the natural colorings of the wild counterparts.

Quick Tip: My pick for a light but delightful seasoning on salmon fillets is Chef of the Future Cajun. You may think of Cajun seasoning as being pretty spicy, but that's not always the case. Chef of the Future is a case in point. The seasoning is balanced and complex, but it is subtle and doesn't overpower the salmon.

Chef of the Future seasoning can be purchased online at www.chef-ofthefuture.com. The chef who created the Cajun and other seasonings in the line is Robert Simon, and I've been using his blends for about a decade now.

Salmon and Asparagus

Asparagus is one of my all-time favorite vegetables, so I'm excited when I see it arrive in the produce section at our local grocery store. I pick up big bundles throughout the short growing season and really enjoy eating this tasty veggie just about any way, from raw to this special meal that I make with wild-caught salmon. There's just something about the combination of these two wonderful flavors that makes a meal fit for a king—or more likely for company, since we don't have kings out in the middle of the southern U.S.

MAKES: 4 servings | **PREP TIME:** 10 minutes | **GRILL TIME:** 25 minutes | **REST TIME:** 2 minutes
Foil needed: 8 (12 x 12-inch) pieces

2 tablespoons olive oil

1 tablespoon orange juice

1 teaspoon honey

½ teaspoon dried rosemary leaves

1 pound fresh asparagus, tough ends trimmed

4 (6-ounce) salmon fillets, preferably wild-caught

salt and pepper, to taste

1. In a small bowl, combine the olive oil, orange juice, honey, and rosemary.

2. Set out 4 pieces of aluminum foil and divide the trimmed asparagus stalks among them.

3. Arrange a salmon fillet on top of each asparagus bundle.

4. Drizzle the olive oil mixture over the salmon and asparagus, dividing equally.

5. Top each salmon pack with a second sheet of foil and seal along all the edges.

6. Grill over medium-high heat for 25 minutes, turning occasionally.

7. Let rest 2 minutes, then cut into the foil and peel it back. Serve immediately, seasoning with salt and pepper.

Fun Fact: Salmon are special fish. While most kinds of fish live in either fresh or saltwater, salmon are anadromous—they live in both types of water. Salmon start out as fish eggs in mountain streams, swim downstream to saltwater, and then return to fresh water to spawn the next generation.

Shrimp Scampi

I live inland, and I still remember the first time I was served shrimp when I was living overseas. Instead of the pile of breaded popcorn shrimp I was used to, several huge shrimp stared up at me. It was a bit disconcerting, I must say. But I dived in—and fell in love.

Fresh shrimp, heads on, is delicious! If you can buy it as it comes straight off the boat, it should be super fresh; just look at the eyes to make sure they are still bright black. You can also smell it—fresh shrimp should have a sweet (not stinky) odor. You may not have access to fresh shrimp, and if you do, it's likely to be quite expensive. To get around this, buy frozen shrimp and let it thaw in the refrigerator.

Serve this dish with pasta and crusty bread for an authentic scampi experience or enjoy it with your favorite campfire vegetables.

Foil needed: 2 (12 x 12-inch) pieces

½ pound large uncooked shrimp with shells (31/35 count, or 31 to 35 per pound)

2 tablespoons (1¼ sticks) butter

1 tablespoon dry, white wine

1 teaspoon lemon juice

1 teaspoon crushed red pepper flakes

1 tablespoon chopped fresh parsley

salt and pepper, to taste

1. Lightly spray a foil sheet with nonstick cooking spray.

2. Place the shrimp, with shells, in the center of the foil.

3. Melt the butter in a small saucepan. Stir in the wine, lemon juice, pepper flakes, parsley, and salt and pepper.

4. Drizzle the butter mixture evenly over the shrimp.

5. Place the second sheet of foil over the top and seal on all sides.

6. Grill for 8 minutes over high heat.

7. Remove from the heat, let rest for 5 minutes, and serve.

Quick Tip: There's no set standard when it comes to the listed size of shrimp. The best indication you are likely to get is the number of shrimp per pound. Most frozen, bagged shrimp and loose shrimp sold at U.S. grocery stores are identified by the number of shrimp per pound. When you see 31/35, for example, that means that there should be 31 to 35 shrimp in a pound.

Shrimp with Veggies

These packs make me feel like I'm at the beach even when I'm inland. I like to serve the shrimp and veggies over rice with slices of Texas toast heated on the grill grates. A big glass of sweet tea rounds out one of my favorite foil meals.

MAKES: 2 servings | **PREP TIME:** 10 minutes | **GRILL TIME:** 15 minutes | **REST TIME:** 5 minutes

Foil needed: 2 (12 x 18-inch) pieces

1 pound large uncooked shrimp

1 pound button mushrooms washed, trimmed

1 large green bell pepper, diced

1 small purple onion, diced

1 tablespoon olive oil

juice from 1 lemon slice

1 teaspoon minced garlic

salt and pepper, to taste

1. Place all the ingredients except salt and pepper in a large zip-top plastic bag. Shake until the contents are evenly distributed.

2. Place half of the shrimp mixture in the center of each piece of foil.

3. Pull the foil edges up over the center in a tent fold and crimp together. Roll up both ends and seal.

4. Grill for 15 minutes over high heat, or until the shrimp is opaque.

5. Let rest for 5 minutes, then use a knife to puncture the pack to release the steam. Pour off the excess moisture and season to taste with salt and pepper.

Quick Tip: If you are using frozen shrimp, don't defrost them in the microwave. Shrimp thaw very quickly, and the microwave will make them growth factories for bacteria. It will also impact their texture and flavor. You really do not want to go there.

A better alternative is to simply run cold water over your frozen shrimp. Put them in a colander and shake it a couple of times as the cold water flows through.

Sauerkraut and Sausage

My dad planted a blessed plenty of cabbage one year, and he and my mom made enough sauerkraut to feed the entire town. I guess some kids would have burned out on sauerkraut, but I found that the more I ate, the more I liked it. It was an easy stretch to start making sauerkraut and sausage foil packages. This is a hearty meal that is especially enjoyable as the days get cooler. Serve with foil roasted potatoes to complete the menu.

MAKES: 1 serving | **PREP TIME:** 10 minutes | **GRILL TIME:** 30 minutes | **REST TIME:** 5 minutes

Foil needed: 2 (12 x 12-inch) pieces

1 cup canned sauerkraut, drained but not rinsed

1 kielbasa sausage link, cut in 1-inch pieces (approximately 4 ounces)

1 tablespoon minced apple

1 tablespoon minced green pepper

1 tablespoon beer

1. Place the drained sauerkraut on the first sheet of foil, spreading it out to make a good base for the sausage.

2. Distribute the kielbasa pieces on top of the sauerkraut.

3. Sprinkle on the apple and green pepper, then the beer.

4. Top with the second sheet of foil and seal well on all sides.

5. Grill over medium heat for 30 minutes.

6. Let rest for 5 minutes and then serve.

Fun Fact: Sauerkraut is the German word for sour cabbage. Although sauerkraut is popular in Germany, where it is usually served with sausages, it didn't originate there. Scholars think that fermented cabbage likely was developed in China, and then the process was imported to Europe. It provided a way to keep cabbage over the winter, purportedly offering a number of health benefits as well.

Beer Brats

Beer brats are a crowd pleaser. I'm always asked why my brats taste so good. Simmering them on the grill in beer with butter and onions is the trick. It also helps to finish the brats off on the grill grates to get a little crunchy contrast in flavor. The brats are fully cooked and heated through after being in the beer simmering, so the direct fire is just to give that extra eye and taste appeal. In this case, the grill marks really do matter.

MAKES: 5 servings | **PREP TIME:** 10 minutes | **GRILL TIME:** 25 minutes plus 5 minutes on grates | **REST TIME:** serve immediately

Foil needed: 1 (12 x 9-inch) pan and 1 (12 x 12-inch) piece

1 pack brat sausages (5 count)

2 (12-ounce) beers

water, to cover sausages

4 tablespoons (½ stick) butter

1 white onion, sliced crosswise and separated into rings

hoagie rolls and prepared mustard, for serving

1. Place the brats in the foil pan and pour the beer over them. Add as much water as needed to barely cover the brats.

2. Add the butter and onion rings to the pan with the brats.

3. Cover the pan with the foil piece, sealing it to the pan edges.

4. Grill over medium heat for 25 minutes, stirring occasionally. You don't want a full boil—aim for a simmer, with very little actual boiling.

5. Remove the foil cover, carefully remove the pan from the grill, and transfer the brats onto the grill grates. Grill for about 5 minutes, or until the sausages have grill marks or are as dark as you want them.

6. Serve immediately on hoagie buns, with mustard.

Breakfast Sausage with Apples

If you live in apple country or even close, you likely look forward to heading out in the fall to get baskets of fresh apples. While most foods aren't purchased by the bushel, apples are so versatile that a basket of apples doesn't last all that long—at least around here.

One of my family's favorite ways to start a day is with an apple dish, and this is one of our best. The contrasting tastes of the sweet-tart apples and the savory sausage links wake up the taste buds as well as the body for a great beginning to the day. Just add a cup of coffee, and you're set.

MAKES: 1 serving | **PREP TIME:** 10 minutes | **GRILL TIME:** 30 minutes | **REST TIME:** 5 minutes

Foil needed: 2 (12 x 9-inch) pieces

½ tablespoon butter

1 large baking apple, cored and diced

8 small precooked breakfast sausage links

1 tablespoon maple syrup, plus extra for serving

⅛ teaspoon crushed red pepper flakes

1. Rub the butter over the center of a foil piece, then distribute the apple pieces over the butter and add the sausages.

2. Drizzle the maple syrup over the apple pieces. Sprinkle on the red pepper flakes.

3. Cover with the second sheet of foil and seal on all sides.

4. Grill for 30 minutes over medium-high heat.

5. Let rest for 5 minutes, then carefully puncture the foil to allow the steam to escape.

6. Serve with additional maple syrup.

Quick Tip: Breakfast sausages are available both raw and cooked. I use cooked links for this recipe to be sure that the sausage will be cooked through. Also, the extra grease from raw sausages can be a bit much in a foil package. If you do have raw sausages, you may want to put them on the grates to cook down and brown a bit before cooking them as directed in this recipe.

Breakfast Casserole

Eggs can be difficult to grill or cook outdoors, where the temperature doesn't remain constant. Variations in heat level just don't work for most egg dishes.

There is good news, though. This breakfast casserole is a pretty sure bet for a filling breakfast that turns out right and tastes great. The key is to make sure the grilling space is good and hot, and as evenly heated as possible.

This breakfast casserole can be assembled the night before and refrigerated. Just be sure to cover the top. Then remove it from the refrigerator and let sit for about 10 minutes before grilling to come closer to room or outdoor temperature. Add about 5 minutes to the grilling time.

MAKES: 4 servings | **PREP TIME:** 15 minutes | **GRILL TIME:** 30 minutes | **REST TIME:** 5 minutes
Foil needed: 1 (12 x 9-inch) pan and 1 (12 x 9-inch) piece

6 slices of day-old bread

6 eggs

1 cup whole milk

1½ cups shredded cheddar cheese

½ pound bulk breakfast sausage, fried and drained

1 cup raw vegetables (mushrooms, green peppers, onions, broccoli, or a combination), cut in bite-size pieces

salt and pepper, to taste

1. Spray the pan with nonstick cooking spray. Set aside.

2. Tear the bread in bite-size pieces and sprinkle evenly in the bottom of the foil pan.

3. In a medium bowl, beat the eggs with a fork. Add the milk and cheese and mix well.

4. Gently fold in the sausage and vegetables.

5. Pour the egg mixture over the bread in the foil pan.

6. Seal the top of the pan with the foil sheet.

7. Grill for 20 minutes over medium heat. Remove the foil sheet and continue grilling for 10 more minutes, or until the eggs look set.

8. Remove from the heat and let rest for 5 minutes.

9. Serve, passing salt and pepper for seasoning to individual tastes.

SIDE DISHES

Apple and Cranberries

As the days get longer, I especially enjoy cooking festive recipes. Apples with cranberries always make me think of Thanksgiving and Christmas, even though apples and dried cranberries are available all year. I grew up with apples served in sweet dishes and cranberries served as an accompaniment to savory foods. Combined, the contrasting flavors of the two fruits pack a nice punch.

This dish serves double duty. Offer it as an accompaniment to ham or turkey, or serve it as a dessert. Either way, it will smell amazing as it cooks on the grill.

MAKES: 1 serving | **PREP TIME:** 10 minutes | **GRILL TIME:** 25 minutes | **REST TIME:** 5 minutes

Foil needed: 1 (12 x 9-inch) piece

1 tablespoon butter

1 medium Fuji apple, cored and sliced

½ cup dried cranberries

1 tablespoon brown sugar

1 teaspoon cinnamon

1. Coat the center of the foil piece with the butter and arrange the apple slices on top.

2. Scatter the cranberries over and around the apple slices, then sprinkle the brown sugar and cinnamon evenly over the fruit.

3. Bring the sides of the foil together and seal, then seal the ends.

4. Grill over medium heat for 25 minutes, turning a couple of times.

5. Let rest for 5 minutes before opening the foil pack.

Fun Fact: You may think that cranberries grow in water, but that's actually a myth. Cranberries grow on vines in marshy, boggy areas. Farmers do flood their fields with water to make harvesting easier. The berries float, making it much less difficult to find and harvest them.

Hasselback Foil Potatoes

You will get some camp cred if you crank out Hasselback potatoes. They are showy and taste divine. If you don't feel quite that inspired, you can always cut a single slit down the center of your potato, add seasonings and a wedge of onion, and do a basic potato. Heck, you can just poke fork holes in a plain potato (so it won't explode), wrap it in foil, and grill it. Potatoes are just easy like that. People do notice the extra effort though, and Hasselbacking your potatoes is worth the extra effort.

MAKES: 1 serving (repeat for each camper) | **PREP TIME:** 10 minutes | **GRILL TIME:** 1 hour and 20 minutes | **REST TIME:** 10 minutes

Foil needed: 1 (12-inch) piece

1 baking potato

1 small purple onion, cut in very thin slices

1 tablespoon butter

1¼ teaspoons powdered garlic

salt and pepper, to taste

1. Slice the potato into ¹⁄₁₆-inch slices without cutting through the bottom. The potato will resemble an accordion when you are done.

2. Gently open to insert onion slices between the slices.

3. Cut the butter in small pieces and press between the potato slices and/or on the outside of the potato.

4. Sprinkle the outside with garlic.

5. Crunch-wrap the aluminum foil around the potato.

6. Grill over medium-high heat for 1 hour and 20 minutes, or until done. Use a fork to check for doneness near the end of the grilling time; simply nudge the foil back and slip in the fork. The potato flesh will feel soft when done.

7. Season with salt and pepper.

Fun Fact: Hasselback potatoes originated in Stockholm, Sweden, at the Hasselbacken Restaurant and Hotel, which is still in operation. The restaurant dates back to the 1700s, but at that time many people thought potatoes were poisonous, so scholars think that Hasselbacks likely date to the 1950s. Like much of food history, you will hear a number of different stories, but one thing is certain—people were impressed with Hasselbackpotatis and loved how they tasted.

Campfire Sweet Potato

My younger son adores sweet potatoes, which he has always called orange potatoes. I'd ask what vegetable he wanted with a meal, and he would grin and say, "Orange potato." While he liked sweet potatoes cooked any way, his favorite was always a basic baked sweet potato, especially one cooked in the campfire. It's super easy to make campfire sweet potatoes. You do need to allow more time for whole potatoes than for most foil package dishes, but it's definitely worth the extra minutes.

MAKES: 1 serving (repeat for each person) | **PREP TIME:** 5 minutes | **GRILL TIME:** 1 hour | **REST TIME:** 10 minutes

Foil needed: 2 (12 x 9-inch) pieces

1 sweet potato

2 tablespoons (1¼ sticks) butter

1 tablespoon brown sugar

1. Stack the foil sheets to make a double-thickness pack.

2. Cut the sweet potato lengthwise down the center without cutting through the bottom.

3. Press the butter and brown sugar into the cut and over the skin of the potato.

4. Crunch-wrap the foil around the sweet potato, making sure that no skin is showing.

5. Place in the campfire, to the edge of white-hot coals.

6. Flip and rotate the potato occasionally. At about 45 minutes, gently wedge the foil open and pierce with a fork to test for doneness; the potato is done when the fork slides in easily. Continue to cook until done, usually about 1 hour.

7. Transfer the foil-wrapped sweet potato to a plate and let rest for about 10 minutes.

8. Carefully push the foil back to release the steam, then slide the potato out onto a plate. Carefully pour the juices from the foil over the sweet potato.

Country Hash Brown Potatoes (Butter Taters)

Our friend Navy Davey turned my family on to "butter taters." On one visit to California where he was previously stationed, he cranked up the grill and loaded up an aluminum foil pan with his "world famous" hash browns grilled with peppers and onions. But the secret ingredient, I'd have to say, was the copious amount of butter.

When we grill these Country Hash Brown Potatoes, we use a little less butter. (Okay—I cut it in half.) But we still get the burst of flavor that has made this a top pick with our family.

MAKES: 8 or more servings | **PREP TIME:** 15 minutes | **GRILL TIME:** 35 minutes |
REST TIME: serve immediately

Foil needed: 1 (9 x 12 x 2-inch) pan and 1 (12 x 18-inch) piece

1 (2-pound) bag frozen country-style diced hash browns

2 large bell peppers (any color), diced

1 medium onion, diced

pepper and Lawry's seasoning salt, to taste

4 tablespoons (½ stick) butter, cut in small pieces

1. Pour the entire bag of hash browns into the aluminum foil pan.

2. Stir in the diced bell peppers and onion. Sprinkle the seasoning salt and pepper over the mixture.

3. Dot the top of the hash browns with the butter pieces.

4. Place the sheet of foil over the top of the pan and seal the edges.

5. Grill for 35 minutes over medium-high, using a turner to move the potatoes around in the pan several times while the dish is grilling.

6. Serve as soon as the hash browns are cooked to the desired crispiness.

Quick Tip: Butter taters are especially tasty if they are crispy in spots. The trick is to release steam toward the end of the cooking time. This can be done either by venting the foil on top or by removing it entirely for the last 10 minutes of cooking time. Let the potatoes sit in the pan long enough to crisp, then stir or turn them so that un-browned portions are exposed to the pan bottom.

Garlic Lemon Potatoes

When I moved to Greece as a young military wife, I discovered that kitchen cooking there was a bit complicated. I lived out "on the economy" in a small fishing village, and I could neither read nor speak Greek. Produce and meats were measured with the metric system. Foods were sold in season rather than being available all year.

One of my favorite dishes during this period was Greek potatoes. My landlady didn't speak English, so I couldn't ask her how to make the delicious tubers she served. But after eating Greek potatoes a few times, I had a pretty good idea as to the included ingredients.

My very first try was a success! I used fresh local potatoes along with lemon and garlic, which are popular flavorings throughout Greece. Then I sealed everything in a foil pan with aluminum foil on top, and I cooked the potatoes on my small tailgate grill. The result was terrific—my potatoes tasted very much like those made by my landlady.

Foil needed: 1 (9 x 9-inch) pan and 1 (12 x 9-inch) piece

6 Yukon Gold potatoes, cut in 1-inch chunks

⅛ cup olive oil

¾ cup water

1 tablespoon minced garlic

1 tablespoon lemon juice

pepper, to taste

chopped, fresh parsley flakes, for garnish

1. In a medium bowl, combine the potatoes, oil, water, garlic, and lemon juice.

2. Transfer the mixture to a 1-gallon zip-top plastic bag, seal, and shake to coat the potatoes evenly.

3. Empty the potatoes into the aluminum foil pan and sprinkle with the pepper and parsley flakes.

4. Seal the top of the pan with the foil piece, crimping the edges tightly.

5. Grill over medium-high heat for 45 minutes.

6. Remove the foil and cook for another 15 minutes, or until the excess moisture has cooked off and the potatoes begin to brown on the bottom.

7. Let rest for 5 minutes before serving.

Fun Fact: Garlic, a highly prized tuber in Greece, is a member of the onion family. In addition to being used to flavor foods, it is thought to have a number of medicinal properties—helping cardiovascular flow, easing digestive distress, fighting infection, and curing leprosy. Garlic was once thought to give Olympic athletes an advantage and increase the stamina of Greek and Roman soldiers on the battlefield.

Bacon Corn

I was hypnotized by beautiful internet photos of bacon-wrapped corn on the cob. But when I tried to make it, the bacon shriveled up and had alternating burned and raw spots. Not good. Using the foil-packet technique was the cure for my sad-looking and sad-tasting grilled bacon corn. The trick is to cook the food in the foil and then flash-brown the bacon over high heat. It sounds complicated, but it's an easy technique to master.

MAKES: 1 serving | **PREP TIME:** 10 minutes | **GRILL TIME:** 35 minutes | **REST TIME:** 5 minutes

Foil needed: 1 (12 x 8-inch) piece

1 ear of corn

1 teaspoon crushed Aleppo pepper

2 slices uncooked bacon

1 teaspoon chopped fresh parsley

1. Sprinkle the pepper evenly over the corn.

2. Carefully wrap the bacon around the ear of corn. Hold it in place while you sprinkle on the parsley. (A helper is handy for this.)

3. Place the corn on the foil and crunch-wrap to seal.

4. Grill over medium-high heat for 30 minutes, turning twice.

5. Gently remove the corn from the foil and place it directly on the grill grates for 3 to 5 minutes until the bacon is crispy, turning once.

6. Let rest for 5 minutes and serve.

Fun Fact: People tend to eat corn on the cob in one of two ways; they eat the kernels a few rows at a time across the cob, or they eat around and around the cob. While it's possible to change corn-eating patterns, almost everyone goes back to their favored pattern when not focused on the question. This is likely related to the question of which way toilet paper should be placed on the holder, flap under or over. The mysteries of the world are never-ending.

Garden Beans and Baby Potatoes

We live in a farming community, and it's always exciting when the beans and new potatoes are ready. There are endless varieties of both, although grocery store options are pretty limited. That's okay, though, because fresh beans and new potatoes taste great regardless of the variety. These summer vegetables shine on their own, so this is a basic way to cook them in foil. You can add other seasonings or fats such as chunks of bacon, ham, or fatback, but flavor boosters are not required.

MAKES: 1 serving | **PREP TIME:** 20 minutes | **GRILL TIME:** 25 minutes | **REST TIME:** 5 minutes

Foil needed: 1 (12 x 12-inch) piece

1¾ cups fresh green beans, stringed and ends snapped

4 new, baby, or fingerling potatoes

1 small onion, sliced crosswise and separated into rings

1 tablespoon olive oil

salt and pepper, to taste

2 ice cubes

1. Place the beans on the sheet of foil, then layer the potatoes and onion slices on top of the beans.

2. Drizzle the olive oil over the beans and potatoes.

3. Season with salt and pepper.

4. Set the ice cubes on top of the food and seal the foil edges together.

5. Grill over medium heat, grill lid closed, for 25 minutes.

6. Let rest for 5 minutes before unwrapping.

Fun Fact: Potatoes come in a variety of colors, from common white to yellow, blue, and red. Sometimes only the peels are colored, but you can also find potatoes that are colored throughout. While they all taste similar, there are some variations of flavor with the different colors. I've also found that blue potatoes take a bit longer to cook than other varieties.

Grilled Pork and Beans

My mother really didn't like to cook. She made pretty basic dishes and generally heated up canned foods. She did, however, get a little fancy with her baked beans. She would pull out various ingredients to "doctor up" the beans. Although she never had a specific recipe, this version is similar to the beans I enjoyed at cookouts when I was growing up. I think you will enjoy these classic beans, too.

MAKES: About 8 servings | **PREP TIME:** 5 minutes | **GRILL TIME:** 1 hour | **REST TIME:** 5 minutes

Foil needed: 1 (9 x 9-inch) pan and 1 (12 x 12-inch) piece

2 (15-ounce) cans pork and beans

1 small onion, diced

1¼ cups molasses

1 tablespoon prepared mustard

2 tablespoons ketchup

1. Pour the beans into the foil pan and stir.

2. Add the onion, molasses, mustard, and ketchup; stir well.

3. Cover with the foil piece and seal it to the sides of the pan.

4. Grill over medium heat for about 1 hour, or until hot and bubbly. Stir every 10 or 15 minutes.

5. Let rest for 5 minutes to allow the sauce to thicken a bit.

Quick Tip: You can make baked beans in individual foil packs, but it's harder to get the flavors and temperature just right. It's just easier to make a pan of beans that will feed a small crowd or can be used as leftovers.

Succotash

The vibrant colors of succotash always make me smile. The flavors make me eat!

In my part of the country, succotash is traditionally made up of tomatoes, corn, and lima beans. If you go farther north, different types of beans are used. That's because lima beans are a Southern crop that needs warm weather. But no matter what type of bean or what extra ingredients you use, succotash is a delightful end-of-summer dish. It's a favorite at my house, and I'm glad I can quickly grill up a batch in foil.

MAKES: 1 serving | **PREP TIME:** 5 minutes | **GRILL TIME:** 15 minutes | **REST TIME:** 5 minutes

Foil needed: 2 (12 x 12-inch) pieces

1 slice bacon, crisp-fried and crumbled, with 2 teaspoons bacon fat reserved*

½ cup drained, canned niblet, shoepeg, or summer corn

½ cup drained, canned lima beans

½ cup canned petite diced tomatoes

salt and pepper, to taste

*If making multiple single packs, fry all the pieces at once.

1. Place the bacon fat in the center of the foil piece.

2. In a small bowl, combine the corn, lima beans, and tomatoes. Stir until evenly mixed, then scatter the crumbled bacon pieces on top.

3. Cover with the second piece of foil and seal tightly on all sides.

4. Grill over medium heat for 15 minutes, or until heated through.

5. Let rest for 5 minutes, then season to taste with salt and pepper.

White Beans with Country Ham

My Poppaw—my grandpa—loved beans. He also loved to recite the little rhyme about the "musical fruit." Although my Poppaw is no longer with us, we still enjoy eating these beans with country ham.

Using canned beans makes this recipe super easy. You are really just heating up the beans and adding flavorings. But don't be fooled by how simple this is to make—it's delicious, and it gives you a wallop of protein. For a true Southern feel, serve with cornbread and sweet iced tea.

MAKES: 1 serving | **PREP TIME:** 5 minutes | **GRILL TIME:** 12 minutes | **REST TIME:** 5 minutes
Foil needed: 1 (12 x 12-inch) piece

1 (15-ounce) can white beans, drained, unrinsed

1 teaspoon Louisiana hot sauce (or other favorite hot sauce)

1 thin slice country ham, cut in bite-size pieces

salt and pepper, to taste

1. Pour the beans onto the center of the foil piece.

2. Splash the hot sauce evenly over the beans and stir gently to distribute evenly.

3. Add the ham pieces and again lightly stir.

4. Grill over medium heat for 12 minutes, or until the beans are heated through.

5. Let cool for 5 minutes, then season with salt and pepper to taste.

Fun Fact: In the South, people (especially of a certain age) may say that they need to buy "seasoning." This may sound vague, but older Southerners use the word "seasoning" to mean salted meat that's used to add flavor. Most often the meat of choice is fatback, which is pure "hard fat" from the pig's back. Other "seasonings" may include bacon and country ham; both are fatty and salty and add a lot of flavor. Younger Southerners will more often season with belly and rump fats.

Portobello Mushroom

My uncle used to hunt mushrooms. Since no one in the family was interested in them, he would take his haul to the home of an elderly lady who would cook up a "mess" of shrooms in exchange for whatever was left over.

I so wish I had gone mushroom hunting with my uncle and had tried his forage crop. At the time, I wasn't very excited about the wild mushrooms he gathered—probably because I'd only had canned mushrooms, which do not taste remotely the same.

Today I do love mushrooms. All types. One of my favorites to grill in foil is portabella. Its large size makes it easy to work with, and it has a rich, earthy flavor. I get my portabellas at the local grocery store, but my mind wanders back to the mountains where my uncle harvests them.

MAKES: 1 serving | **PREP TIME:** 5 minutes | **GRILL TIME:** 10 minutes | **REST TIME:** serve immediately
Foil needed: 2 (12 x 9-inch) pieces

1 large portobello mushroom cap (or 2 if they are small)

2 teaspoons olive oil

⅛ teaspoon crushed red pepper flakes

1 tablespoon chopped fresh parsley

salt and pepper, to taste

1. Brush the mushroom all over with the olive oil.

2. Place the mushroom in the center of the foil sheet and sprinkle all over with pepper flakes, parsley, and salt and pepper.

3. Top with the second foil sheet and seal all the edges.

4. Grill over medium heat for 10 minutes, flipping the packet over at about 6 minutes.

5. Carefully puncture the pack to release the steam before opening.

Fun Fact: Many of the mushrooms you see at the grocery store are really the same type, just at different levels of maturity. The small button or baby bella mushrooms are just younger versions of the more mature portobello mushrooms, which are allowed to grow longer and get darker as they grow.

Bacon Brussels Sprouts

Usually even people who think they don't like Brussels sprouts fall in love with them done this way in foil packets. Sweet and salty combine for a dish that seems more gourmet than campfire.

MAKES: 2 servings | **PREP TIME:** 20 minutes | **GRILL TIME:** 25 minutes | **REST TIME:** 5 minutes

Foil needed: 1 (12 x 12-inch) piece

2 tablespoons olive oil

2 tablespoons maple syrup

2 slices crisp-fried bacon, with 1 tablespoon bacon fat reserved

1 teaspoon sea salt

½ teaspoon freshly ground pepper

10 medium Brussels sprouts

1. Combine the olive oil, maple syrup, bacon fat, salt, and pepper in a zip-top plastic bag. Seal the bag and mash with your hands until the ingredients are evenly distributed.

2. Add the Brussels sprouts to the bag and massage to evenly coat them with the olive oil mixture.

3. Pour the Brussels sprouts onto the foil sheet. Crumble the bacon slices and add on top of Brussels sprouts and seal the edges closed.

4. Grill over medium heat, grill lid closed, for 25 minutes.

5. Let rest for 5 minutes, then unseal and serve.

Quick Tip: You can use frozen Brussels sprouts for this recipe. (Start with frozen sprouts, not thawed, and double the grilling time.) However, they aren't nearly as good as the fresh ones.

When you see Brussels sprouts in the store during their peak autumn harvest season, take the opportunity to make any recipes you've been saving. Flavor-wise, it's best to use your Brussels sprouts within three days of purchase, if you can. It's okay to store them in the refrigerator for up to a week, but they will become more bitter and less sweet as they sit in storage.

Rigani Squash Packs (Greek Oregano Squash Packs)

We grow summer squash in our garden, and in season the plants produce like rabbits. A single plant would feed everyone on our road. The family loves fried squash, but that's not the healthiest option, and it's a lot of work. This foil package is lighter in fats and calories but still big on flavor. Since I lived in Greece for a while as a member of a military family, the Mediterranean twist just seemed like a natural.

MAKES: 2 servings | **PREP TIME:** 15 minutes | **GRILL TIME:** 15 minutes | **REST TIME:** serve immediately

Foil needed: 1 (12 x 12-inch) piece

1½ cups summer squash, cut in 1¼-inch circles

2 teaspoons olive oil

1 teaspoon garlic granules

1 teaspoon dried rigani (Greek oregano)

½ cup crumbled feta cheese

1. Put the squash in a quart-size zip-top plastic bag.

2. Add the olive oil, garlic, and oregano, then gently massage the bag until the squash is evenly coated with the seasonings.

3. Transfer the mixture onto the piece of foil, top with the feta cheese, and seal.

4. Grill over medium heat, grill lid closed, for 15 minutes. Serve immediately after removing from the heat.

Quick Tip: Greek oregano, or rigani, is considered the "true" oregano. It's what most people think of when the herb is mentioned, and most oreganos sold at the grocery store are Greek. If you grow your own oregano or can find fresh leaves, scale back on the amount in the recipe by half. Fresh rigani is quite spicy—so spicy, in fact, that it can make the tip of your tongue feel numb. A little goes a long way.

Sesame Asparagus

Heaven, for me, was living in an old farmhouse with a huge asparagus patch out back. I'd sit at the edge of the asparagus bed and eat the stalks raw. Getting an asparagus bed established takes a lot of time and work, so I've never put one in at our current home. I do, however, keep an eye out for when fresh asparagus comes into season in late spring or early summer. I buy lots and really enjoy making this delicious seasonal dish in foil.

MAKES: 4 servings | **PREP TIME:** 15 minutes | **GRILL TIME:** 10 to 15 minutes | **REST TIME:** 5 minutes
Foil needed: 1 (12 x 12-inch) piece

1 pound fresh asparagus, tough ends trimmed

1 tablespoon sesame oil

2 tablespoons soy sauce

2 tablespoons honey

1 teaspoon sesame seeds

sea salt and pepper, to taste

1 cup shredded mozzarella cheese (optional)

1. Arrange the asparagus in a single layer on the foil.

2. Drizzle the sesame oil over the asparagus.

3. Mix the soy sauce, honey, and sesame seeds in a small bowl and pour over the asparagus. Sprinkle on salt and pepper according to taste, then seal the foil closed.

4. Grill over medium-high heat, grill lid closed, for 10 to 15 minutes depending on the thickness of the stalks.

5. Let rest for 5 minutes, then carefully open and sprinkle cheese evenly over the asparagus, if using. Serve when the cheese has melted.

Quick Tip: The ends of asparagus stalks are mealy and tough. People often ask me how much to cut off. What you want to do is bend the stalks; they will bend right where they go from being delicious to being tough. Just put a little pressure on the stalks while holding the top ends in one hand and the bottom ends in the other and cut the bottoms off where you see them naturally bend. You'll have this down pat after you've done it once, and you'll be rocking the fresh asparagus.

Italian Cauliflower

If you want a big, showy side dish, Italian cauliflower is the ticket. It draws attention on the grill due to its large size, and it's quite splashy when done. Although this is a rather large item to grill, the spaces within the cauliflower head make for fairly quick grilling.

MAKES: About 6 servings | **PREP TIME:** 10 minutes | **GRILL TIME:** 45 minutes | **REST TIME:** 5 minutes

Foil needed: 2 (12 x 12-inch) pieces

1 head cauliflower

2 tablespoons olive oil

2 teaspoons Italian seasoning

1 teaspoon paprika

1 slice onion

1¼ teaspoons sea salt

pepper, to taste

1. Trim back the leaves on the cauliflower and set the head on a foil sheet.

2. Drizzle olive oil evenly over the cauliflower, then sprinkle on the Italian seasoning and paprika.

3. Place the onion slice on top of the cauliflower.

4. Sprinkle sea salt and pepper over the cauliflower.

5. Wrap the foil up and around the sides of the cauliflower. Then crunch-wrap the second sheet of foil over the top and down over the bottom sheet.

6. Grill over medium heat, grill lid closed, for 45 minutes.

7. Let rest for 5 minutes, then unwrap and serve.

Quick Tip: To stabilize a wobbly head of cauliflower on the grill, you can make a holder of sorts out of aluminum foil. Pull out about 18 inches of foil and then fold and crunch it into a long strip about a half inch wide. Form the strip into a circle a little smaller in diameter than the cauliflower head, then use your fingers to coax the ring of foil under the cauliflower.

Baby Carrots

When I was in college, my advisor had me over for Thanksgiving dinner, since I lived across the country and couldn't go home for the holiday. One of the dishes served was carrots with orange juice. I loved that dish, and I've made versions of it ever since. Baby carrots in aluminum foil is a really tasty side dish, and the aroma is amazing as these treats slowly cook over the fire.

MAKES: 4 servings | **PREP TIME:** 5 minutes | **GRILL TIME:** 40 minutes | **REST TIME:** 5 minutes
Foil needed: 2 (12 x 12-inch) pieces

2 cups baby carrots
1 tablespoon butter
½ tablespoon brown sugar

1 tablespoon orange juice
1 teaspoon ground ginger

1. Combine all the ingredients in a small bowl or a zip-top plastic bag. Mix well.

2. Set out a piece of aluminum foil and transfer the carrot mixture to the center of the foil sheet.

3. Top with the second foil sheet and seal all the edges.

4. Grill for 40 minutes, flipping over once.

5. Let rest for 5 minutes, then open the pack carefully—there will likely be liquid in the bottom—and stir the carrots around in the juice.

Quick Tip: Carrots keep longer than most vegetables. To extend the life of your carrots, don't store them with fruits. Some fruits give off ethylene gas, which will cause your carrots to ripen quickly and to decay faster than they normally would.

SNACKS

Ham Cheese Foil Sliders

I could always count on one of the church ladies to bring ham cheese sandwiches to potluck dinners when I was growing up. This made me happy, because I loved the little sandwiches, which I considered the ultimate in "elegant."

Now I make ham cheese foil-witches pretty much as I had them years ago, but with various breads since there are more options these days. I prefer the flavor of a basic white dinner roll, but many people like Hawaiian rolls for these. I find Hawaiian rolls awfully sweet combined with the ham, but I'm not picky—I'll eat these sandwiches on any type of roll and on any day of the week!

MAKES: 12 sliders | **PREP TIME:** 5 minutes | **GRILL TIME:** 20 minutes | **REST TIME:** serve immediately

Foil needed: 1 piece, 6 inches longer than the bread pan

2 tablespoons (1¼ sticks) butter

2 teaspoons spicy brown mustard

2 teaspoons poppy seeds

1 pan of 12 white dinner rolls in foil pan (or buy a foil pan to fit the rolls in if you don't find them sold in pans)

mayonnaise, to taste

8 slices deli ham

8 slices Swiss cheese

1. In a small pan, melt the butter over the grill. Stir in the mustard and poppy seeds; set aside.

2. Without separating the rolls, remove them from their foil pan. Cut in half cross-wise, like a giant hamburger bun.

3. Place the bottom section back in the pan and spread mayonnaise over the cut surface.

4. Arrange the ham slices on the mayonnaise; you may have some overlap. Place the cheese slices over the ham slices. Again, they may overlap.

5. Place the top section of rolls back in the pan, covering the ham and cheese.

6. Pour the butter mixture evenly over the tops of the rolls.

7. Wrap the foil sheet loosely over the top of the pan to prevent burning and moisture buildup and crimp loosely around the pan edges.

8. Grill over medium heat for 20 minutes, or until the cheese has melted and the butter has soaked into the roll tops.

9. Remove from the grill, remove the foil sheet, and use a serrated knife to cut into pieces along the original roll sections. Serve immediately.

Fun Fact: You may have heard the urban legend that eating poppy seeds can make you fail a drug test. Guess what? That's fact. Poppies are the base ingredient for morphine. Although you don't get a "high" from eating poppy seeds, you may get a false positive on a drug test.

Campfire Pizza Pockets

When I was young, pizza was a special treat. I remember gorging on pepperoni pizza at the local pizza parlor and also getting to make boxed pizza with friends on my birthday.

Now pizza is a delivery away. It's easier to order in a pizza than to cook a meal, and it's usually cheaper, too. This is good in some ways, since I do love pizza. But I kind of take it for granted because it's so readily available. One way to make pizza extra special again is to make pizza pockets on camping trips. The flavors are familiar, but the execution and delivery are a bit different.

MAKES: 8 servings for a small group (one pizza pocket each) | **PREP TIME:** 8 to 10 minutes |
GRILL TIME: 15 to 20 minutes | **REST TIME:** 5 minutes

Foil needed: 1 nonstick roll

pita pockets, 1 per camper

1 jar or can of your favorite pizza sauce

1 small package (6 ounce) pepperoni slices

8 ounces shredded pizza cheese

pizza toppings, such as sliced onions, sliced mushrooms, pineapple chunks, sliced olives, or sliced ham

1. For each camper, tear off a piece of foil large enough to hold the pita pocket and fold back over to seal.

2. Cut open space in the pita pockets to fill and distribute one to each camper. You may want to cut them in half if they are large. Smaller servings mean less waste, and they will heat faster.

3. Add a generous spoonful of pizza sauce to each pita pocket. Have campers shake or gently massage their pita shells to distribute the sauce inside.

4. Add a generous amount of cheese and pepperoni to each pita pocket.

5. Let each person select toppings and add them to the pita pocket. Or you can stick with plain sauce and cheese or pepperoni pockets to simplify things.

6. Have the campers center their pita pizzas on their foil pieces, then pull up the sides of the foil like a tent, seal up the tent top, and seal both ends.

7. Using a fork, poke a couple of small holes in the top of the foil pack to release moisture. Too much moisture can make the pizza pocket soggy.

8. Grill over low heat or place next to hot coals (but not right in the coals) for 4 to 5 minutes, then rotate or flip the packs, depending on the heat source. For more direct heat like coals or a fire, you would need to flip the packet. The key is to heat the pita pockets as evenly as possible. Heat for 10 to 15 more minutes or 15 to 20 minutes total.

9. Carefully remove the pita pizzas from the heat and let cool for a few minutes—you don't want anyone's mouth to get burned. Pizza fillings can be hotter than you might expect. Then let everyone enjoy a tasty meal that takes almost no work and requires hardly any cleanup.

Fun Fact: Pizza is different all over the world. Italy offers soft bread crusts with marinara and a little cheese. Japan goes rather wild with the toppings, sometimes using corn as the star. The cheese in Nea Makri was placed on the crust, then the sauce was loaded on top of the cheese.

Even in the United States, different regions interpret pizza quite differently. From crispy-thin, New York pepperoni to deep-dish Chicago-style pies, I've not come across a type of pizza that I didn't like—although I admit to doing a double take over Canadian pizza with pineapple.

Quesadillas

Quesadillas may be the ultimate comfort food. There's just something about the warm tortillas and melty cheese that make even a bad day seem okay.

Quesadillas are super simple to make. You really just need to heat them until the cheese is soft and gooey. If you like additional flavors, you can easily load your quesadillas with your favorite toppings or fillings. Around here, we generally go with the basic version. It's hard to beat.

MAKES: 1 serving | **PREP TIME:** 5 minutes | **GRILL TIME:** 8 minutes | **REST TIME:** serve immediately

Foil needed: 2 (12 x 12-inch) pieces

2 (8-inch) flour tortillas (adjust foil length and cheese amount if using another size)

¾ cup shredded Mexican cheese blend or Monterey Jack cheese

additional fillings, if desired

pico de gallo, salsa, sour cream, or other toppings, for serving

1. Place a flour tortilla in the center of a piece of foil.

2. Spread the cheese evenly over the tortilla.

3. Add any favorite fillings to the cheese and cover with the second tortilla.

4. Top with the second piece of foil and seal the edges together.

5. Grill over medium heat for 8 minutes, or until the cheese is melty. Rotate a couple of times to ensure even heating.

6. Remove from the grill and serve immediately with pico de gallo, salsa, sour cream, or other favorite toppings. It can be eaten whole or cut into pieces.

Quick Tip: Flour tortillas will keep longer if you store them in the refrigerator at below 40°F. The rule of thumb is that they will keep through the package "sell by" date if left out on the counter, and twice that time if refrigerated. Room-temperature tortillas are usually good for a week or two, chilled tortillas for close to a month.

Buffalo Cauliflower Bites

Cauliflower has the texture and crunch to be used like chicken wings with hot sauce. The trick is to be sure the cauliflower florets are coated well and evenly. Then it's just a matter of lightly steaming the dish and serving it piping hot. As the cauliflower pieces cool off, they begin to lose their crunch and aren't as tasty, so be sure to eat them immediately after they are removed from the heat.

MAKES: 4 servings | **PREP TIME:** 15 minutes | **GRILL TIME:** 15 minutes | **REST TIME:** serve immediately

Foil needed: 8 (9 x 12-inch) pieces

1 cauliflower head, broken into bite-size chunks

1¼ cups Louisiana hot sauce (or Frank's Red Hot)

½ cup softened cream cheese

½ cup shredded cheddar cheese

1 tablespoon maple syrup

ranch dressing, for dipping

1. Break the cauliflower into bite-size chunks.

2. Place the hot sauce, cream cheese, cheddar cheese, and maple syrup in a zip-top plastic bag. Seal the bag and mash with your hands until everything is evenly mixed.

3. Add the cauliflower chunks to the bag and gently massage until they are evenly coated with the sauce mixture.

4. Place the pieces evenly on four sheets of foil. Add top layer of foil and seal sides.

5. Grill over medium heat for 14 minutes.

6. Serve immediately, offering the ranch dressing for dipping the hot cauliflower pieces.

Fun Fact: A number of stories are in circulation about the origination of buffalo wings, but most people agree that these snack bites smothered in hot sauce started out at the Anchor Bar in New York City. What's not in question is the popularity of buffalo wings and other spicy bites across the entire United States and, in fact, across much of the globe.

Foil Pan Nacho Chips

I came up with this many years back when I realized that my friends and family liked to snack while I was heating up the grill. It made sense to make something quick and easy. I thought nacho chips would probably work, and they surely did. I've lost count of how many times I've slipped a pan of these onto the grill to tide everyone over until the main course was ready.

MAKES: 4 or more servings | **PREP TIME:** 10 minutes | **GRILL TIME:** 1 to 3 minutes |
REST TIME: serve immediately

Foil needed: 1 (9 x 9 x 1-inch) pan, 1 (12 x 10-inch) piece

tortilla chips to cover the bottom of the foil pan

4 ounces shredded Mexican cheese blend

15 to 20 jalapeño pepper slices

1. Place a single layer of chips in the foil pan. The chips can overlap somewhat but will be cheesier if not completely layered.

2. Arrange the jalapeño slices evenly over the chips, then top with the shredded cheese.

3. Cover the pan with the foil piece, crimping the edges shut.

4. Place over a gas grill as it is preheating for 1 to 3 minutes, or until you hear a faint sizzling sound. Remove from the heat the second the cheese begins to sizzle.

5. Serve immediately.

Quick Tip: You can use all your favorite tortilla toppings on these chips, either under the cheese or on top of it. Some favorites include cooked ground beef, cooked shredded chicken, cooked pulled pork, sliced black olives, and chopped or sliced onions. The only real rule for nachos made on the grill is to be sure that the toppings are precooked or okay raw, since the heating time is so brief.

Mushroom Poppers

You will have happy campers if you pop open a foil pack of these mushroom poppers. The flavor is similar to pizza, so these make a popular snack for all ages. They are simple to make and cook pretty quickly.

MAKES: 4 servings | **PREP TIME:** 15 minutes | **GRILL TIME:** 15 minutes | **REST TIME:** 5 minutes

Foil needed: 2 (12 x 12-inch) pieces

12 baby bella mushrooms (also called crimini or baby portobello)

1 cup salsa

1 cup shredded Mexican cheese blend or cheddar cheese

1 tablespoon taco seasoning

1. Clean the mushrooms and remove the stems. Blot lightly with a paper towel to remove excess moisture.

2. In a small bowl, combine the salsa and cheese, mixing evenly.

3. Using your fingers or a spoon, press small amounts of the salsa/cheese mixture into the stem openings of the mushrooms. Divide evenly among the mushrooms.

4. Spray a foil sheet lightly with nonstick cooking spray. Then place the mushrooms on the foil, filling side up, and evenly sprinkle the taco seasoning over them. Cover with the second sheet of foil and seal the edges.

5. Grill over medium heat for 15 minutes.

6. Remove from the heat and let rest for 5 minutes, then open the foil packet and pour off any accumulated liquid. Serve immediately.

Quick Tip: Be careful when foil-grilling mushrooms. Mushrooms contain a lot of moisture, so you are likely to have liquid in the bottom of the foil pack. Use camping gloves or long-handled tongs to open the foil packets and stand back from the pack to avoid steam and liquid.

Sausage Poppers

When I visit groups to talk about grilling, I like to take something to make for a snack. Everyone loves to eat, after all. Sausage Poppers are a go-to choice because they are easy to prep and grill up quickly. They never get boring, since I vary the seasoning and rub mixtures.

MAKES: 4 servings | **PREP TIME:** 5 minutes | **GRILL TIME:** 8 minutes | **REST TIME:** serve immediately

Foil needed: 1 (12 x 12-inch) piece

4 cups precooked smoked sausage links (about 1 pound)

2 tablespoons barbecue seasoning or rub prepared mustard, for dipping

1. Cut the sausage in bite-size circles about ½ inch thick.

2. Place the sausage rounds and the barbecue seasoning in a gallon-size plastic zip-top bag. Massage the bag to distribute the seasoning evenly.

3. Spray the foil with nonstick cooking spray. Place the sausages on the foil and bring the edges together to seal.

4. Grill over medium heat for 8 minutes.

5. Serve immediately, with toothpicks for dipping the sausage bits into the mustard.

Quick Tip: I like my sausages crispy, but bite-size bits of food on a grate are hard to turn and can fall through into the fire. To get around this, I use a grill wok basket to brown foods such as these sausage bites. Once they are heated in their foil pack, I just pour them into the wok and set them over a direct flame until there are black marks. This takes only about a minute.

Cocktail Snack Bites

When I was growing up, nothing said party like cocktail snacks. I didn't know how these little appetizers were made back then, but I knew that I loved them and that there were never any left over.

I modified this classic recipe so that it could be made over a campfire. These tasty treats were just as popular as I remembered from my childhood. Some things are just hard to beat.

MAKES: 8 or more servings | **PREP TIME:** 5 minutes | **GRILL TIME:** 20 minutes | **REST TIME:** serve immediately

Foil needed: 1 (12 x 9 x 2-inch) pan and 1 (12 x 12-inch) piece

1 cup grape jelly

1 (12-ounce) bottle Heinz Chili Sauce

2 (14-ounce) packages miniature cocktail sausages

1. In the foil pan, mix together the jelly and chili sauce.

2. Add the sausages and stir until they are evenly coated with the sauce.

3. Place the foil sheet over the pan and seal the edges.

4. Grill over medium-low heat for 20 minutes, or until the mixture is hot and shiny.

5. Serve with toothpicks.

Quick Tip: If you can't find chili sauce at your grocery or camp store, you can use barbecue sauce to make this snack. If your barbecue sauce is on the sweet side, you may want to add some heat with a few shakes of hot sauce or a few dashes of red pepper.

Creamy Cheese Dip

My brother introduced me to this dip, and I was hooked from the first bite. The richness of the cheese together with the kick of the hot sauce are just really tasty.

I consider this a dip for a twosome, but I'm sure I could eat a whole pack. Then again, I'm not really known for my restraint. If you want to make a larger batch, you can use an aluminum foil pan and increase the amounts accordingly. You'll also want to lower the heat and increase the heating time to prevent burning.

MAKES: 2 servings | **PREP TIME:** 5 minutes | **GRILL TIME:** 15 minutes | **REST TIME:** 5 minutes

Foil needed: 2 (12 x 18-inch) pieces

1 (4-ounce) container whipped cream cheese

1 tablespoon hot sauce

½ cup cooked chicken, cut in small pieces

1 tablespoon chopped chives

chips or cut-up raw vegetables, for serving

1. Stack the sheets of foil to form a double-layer pack. Lightly spray the foil with nonstick spray.

2. Empty the cream cheese container onto the center of the foil and sprinkle the hot sauce over the top.

3. Stir in the cooked chicken, then top with the chives.

4. Pull the long edges of the doubled foil together like a tent and fold over a couple of times to seal. Roll up the ends to complete the pack.

5. Grill over medium heat for 15 minutes, let rest for 5 minutes, and serve with chips or cut-up vegetables.

Quick Tip: It is helpful to cook a whole chicken and freeze the meat in bags to have on hand for recipes like this. Or you can pick up a rotisserie chicken and break apart the amount you need for any recipe that calls for cooked chicken.

Toasted Nuts

I grew up with a huge pecan tree right outside my bedroom window. I didn't realize how lucky I was until the tree finally had to be cut down due to old age. Yes, trees do get old and begin to die—it's sad, but it's a fact.

When our pecans began to drop each year, we'd have tons of them. We ate some raw, used many in recipes, and froze some. And we had roasted pecans—yum! This snack is a tribute to the toasted pecans that I loved when I was growing up. I do use mixed nuts, since pecans are quite expensive. There are always a few pecans in every can, so I get a quick taste of the past when I grill up a batch. Serve these nuts with beer or apple cider.

MAKES: 2 cups | **PREP TIME:** 2 minutes | **GRILL TIME:** 8 minutes | **REST TIME:** 5 minutes

Foil needed: 2 (12 x 9-inch) pieces

2 cups mixed roasted and salted nuts

1 tablespoon room-temperature butter

1 teaspoon barbecue seasoning/rub

1. Lay out a sheet of foil and pour the nuts onto the center.

2. Cut the butter in small chunks and stir in with the nuts.

3. Add the barbecue seasoning and stir to distribute evenly.

4. Cover with the second foil piece and seal closed on all sides.

5. Grill for 8 minutes over medium heat, turning a couple of times.

6. Let rest for 5 minutes, then serve.

Fun Fact: Cashews are in the same plant family as poison ivy and sumac. Of course, cashew nuts won't hurt you unless you have a tree nut allergy. The shells of cashews do contain oil that can make your skin itch, but you're not likely to see cashews sold in their shells in most countries.

Buttered Pretzels

I noticed that all the pretzels were missing from our holiday party mix. After a little detective work, I figured out that my younger son liked the pretzels way more than the cereal or nuts. Thus was born this buttery pretzels-only snack.

In addition to their salty, buttery flavor, on the grill these Buttered Pretzels also pick up a smoky flavor. Gotta love that. This is a great pick for a good-sized group, and it's also quite cost effective.

MAKES: 8 or more servings | **PREP TIME:** 15 minutes | **GRILL TIME:** 45 minutes | **REST TIME:** 5 minutes
Foil needed: 1 (12 x 9-inch) pan, 1 (12 x 14-inch) piece

3 tablespoons butter
1 tablespoon Worcestershire sauce

¾ teaspoon seasoning salt
6 cups pretzels

1. In a small pan, melt the butter with the Worcestershire sauce and seasoning salt in a small pan on the grill. (Or you can use the aluminum pan for melting if you wear gloves and are very careful.)

2. Pour the pretzels into the aluminum pan, then pour the butter mixture over the pretzels; stir.

3. Cover the pan with the foil piece and seal all the edges.

4. Grill for 15 minutes over medium-low heat. Then loosen the foil, stir the pretzels, and continue grilling for another 15 minutes with the foil loosened.

5. Remove the foil and grill uncovered for another 15 minutes, or until the pretzels are shiny and crispy.

6. Let rest for 5 minutes and then serve.

Quick Tip: You can save and store any leftover pretzels for about a month in a sealed container or plastic bag. Just be sure that they've been grilled long enough that the butter is baked in well. You can tell if you have it right by touching the pretzels—they shouldn't feel greasy. You can also freeze buttered pretzels, extending their life up to six months.

Garlic Cheese Bread

I have loved garlic bread since childhood, when we had white bread slices slathered with butter and sprinkled with garlic salt as a side treat with spaghetti. Today I much prefer deli bread or even home-cooked bread dressed up with butter, cheese, and garlic. Making this when camping makes the bread taste even better, and it's easy to make in foil.

MAKES: About 12 servings | **PREP TIME:** 10 minutes | **GRILL TIME:** 25 minutes | **REST TIME:** serve immediately

Foil needed: 2 pieces, 12 inches longer than the bread loaf

1 loaf white bread (Italian, French, etc.), unsliced

1 (8-ounce) tub spreadable butter

1 (8-ounce) package shredded Parmesan cheese

garlic sprinkles or garlic salt

1. Using a serrated knife, cut the bread into slices about 2 inches thick without cutting through the bottom.

2. Spread butter in the cuts along the entire loaf of bread.

3. Gently wedge the cuts open far enough to sprinkle in cheese.

4. Sprinkle garlic between the slices, then gently press the bread back into shape.

5. Dot a little extra butter on top of the bread.

6. Top with the second sheet of foil. Press the bottom sheet up around the bread and the top sheet down over the bottom sheet. Tuck the ends together and crunch them up close to the loaf ends.

7. Grill over medium heat for 25 minutes, or until the butter and cheese are melted. If you like your bread toasty, lay the unwrapped loaf on the grates for just a couple of minutes. Watch carefully, as the cheese can easily burn.

8. Serve immediately, with a meal or as a snack around the campfire.

Quick Tip: The real trick to making good bread outdoors is to keep the temperature at a low but constant level. If you have the heat too high, the cheese will melt and stick to the foil. If it's too low, the bread will get kind of mushy and take a long time to heat through.

DESSERTS

Apple Bomb

Apple Bombs are fun to make on a campfire but also fine on a grill. They aren't dependent on the foil to hold the steam, since apples have a lot of natural water. This means that it's fine to check the apples for doneness and to continue grilling as needed. Just be careful—use grill gloves to peel back the foil and fork-test the apples. If they don't feel soft enough, carefully press the foil back tight and continue cooking.

MAKES: 1 serving | **PREP TIME:** 15 minutes | **GRILL TIME:** 45 minutes to 1 hour | **REST TIME:** 5 minutes
Foil needed: 1 (12 x 12-inch) piece

1 medium Fuji apple
1 tablespoon butter

1 tablespoon Red Hots candies

1. Core the apple, leaving the bottom intact so the fillings won't spill out.

2. Set the apple on the foil and insert the butter in the center hole. Add the candies, pressing them down into the butter so they will stay in place.

3. Crunch-wrap the foil up and around the apple, with the seam at the top.

4. Grill over medium heat for 45 minutes to 1 hour. Use a fork to check after 45 minutes; the apple should be soft, with just a slight give. If it feels too firm, continue grilling.

5. When done, let rest for 5 minutes and then serve with the foil in place to hold the tasty liquid that puddles under the apple.

Quick Tip: Fuji apples work really well for Apple Bombs, because they are firm but also have sweet notes. If you opt to use a more traditional baking apple such as Granny Smith, you may want to add some brown sugar along with the Red Hots.

Neon Apples

When I was a child, one of the ladies from my church always made Neon Apples for the annual country ham dinner. I thought they were especially pretty. Now that I'm the adult, I like to make Neon Apples in foil packs. They are quick and easy to prepare, and kids really like the colorful presentation.

MAKES: 1 serving | **PREP TIME:** 5 minutes | **GRILL TIME:** 25 | **REST TIME:** 5 minutes

Foil needed: 2 (12 x 12-inch) pieces

1 tablespoon butter

1 baking apple, such as Granny Smith, cored and cut in slices

1 tablespoon strawberry Jell-O powder

1. Place the butter in the center of a foil sheet.

2. Arrange the apple slices on top of the butter and sprinkle with the Jell-O powder.

3. Top with the second foil sheet and seal on all sides.

4. Grill over medium heat for 25 minutes, or until the apple slices are tender.

5. Let rest for 5 minutes, then carefully unwrap.

Quick Tip: I prefer regular strawberry Jell-O for this treat, but it can also be made with other flavors or with sugar-free Jell-O.

Peaches and Blueberries

I live in peach country and always look forward to the peaches ripening each summer. I eat them lots of ways, but this may be my very favorite. Cooking peaches on the grill smell fabulous—and they taste even better.

MAKES: 1 serving | **PREP TIME:** 5 minutes | **GRILL TIME:** 10 minutes | **REST TIME:** 5 minutes

Foil needed: 2 (12 x 9-inch) pieces

1 medium ripe peach, peeled and sliced

1¼ cups fresh blueberries

1 tablespoon butter

1 tablespoon brown sugar, to taste

1. Lightly coat a foil sheet with nonstick spray and put the peach slices in the center of the sheet.

2. Pour the blueberries over the peaches.

3. Cut the butter in small chunks and distribute evenly over the fruit.

4. Sprinkle the sugar evenly over the top.

5. Cover with the second sheet of foil and seal the edges closed.

6. Grill for 10 minutes over medium heat, or until heated through.

7. Let rest for 5 minutes before opening.

Quick Tip: Like most fruits, peaches vary in sweetness depending on the variety, the weather, and when they were picked. If you have very sweet peaches, you may not need to add any sugar. For peaches that don't pack a lot of sweetness, just increase the amount of sugar called for in this recipe.

Pineapple Upside-Down Cakelette

My grandma used to make pineapple upside-down cake, and I loved it. I don't often see it these days, but it's still a delicious treat. Foil-packet pineapple upside-down cakes are a little different from the full-size cakes my grandma baked in cast iron, but they are nonetheless a favorite with campers young and old.

MAKES: 1 serving | **PREP TIME:** 5 minutes | **GRILL TIME:** 15 minutes | **REST TIME:** 5 minutes

Foil needed: 1 (12 x 12-inch) piece

½ tablespoon butter

1 tablespoon light brown sugar

1 pineapple ring

1 maraschino cherry

1 vanilla dessert shell

1. Lightly coat the foil sheet with nonstick cooking spray.

2. Place the butter in the center of the foil; top with the sugar.

3. Add the pineapple ring over the butter and sugar and place the cherry in the center.

4. Position the dessert shell upside down over the pineapple.

5. Seal up the foil on all sides.

6. Grill, pineapple side down, for 15 minutes over medium heat.

7. Let rest for 5 minutes, then invert to serve.

Quick Tip: Dessert shells are displayed near the strawberries in most grocery stores, though they may not be available after the strawberry season wraps up. Dessert shells can be frozen for use later. If you can't find them, you can also use a cake-style doughnut cut in half horizontally. The doughnut needs to be cut like a bagel, allowing for two pieces to be used.

Banana Boats

If your kids love s'mores, this is a fun play on the classic campfire treat but with some fruit for added nutrition. Banana Boats are easy enough for a preschooler to assemble, and they heat quickly enough for even the most impatient camper. Well, there's always one who wanted it an hour ago, but this is one of the fastest foil treats you can make—ready in minutes.

Bite-size candies such as miniature peanut butter cups also work. With a little finesse, creamy full-size soft candies (such as Reese's Peanut Butter Cups) can be cut apart and used in this recipe.

MAKES: 1 serving (repeat for each camper) | **PREP TIME:** 5 minutes | **GRILL TIME:** 6 to 8 minutes | **REST TIME:** 5 minutes

Foil needed: 1 piece, 4 inches longer than the banana

1 banana (barely ripe)

6 miniature marshmallows

6 chocolate chips and 6 peanut butter chips, or 1 chocolate peanut butter cup cut into 4 pieces

1. Holding the banana firmly, cut from end to end without slicing through the bottom of the peel.

2. Use the knife or your fingers to gently wedge the slit open wider. Then use a finger to push the marshmallows, chocolate chips, and peanut butter chips into the slit (don't force it), distributing them evenly along the length of the banana.

3. Push the banana gently back into shape, or as close as you can without pushing the filling out.

4. With the cut side facing up, hold the banana steady (or have someone else hold it) and crunch-wrap the foil around it.

5. Set the foil-wrapped banana on the low-heat side of a gas grill, over dying charcoal grill coals, or to the side of campfire embers. You don't want the banana peel to get too black, which some kids find gross. You'll still get some black coloration, but not as much if you use gentle heat.

6. Let the banana boat heat for 3 to 4 minutes, then turn 180 degrees and heat for another 3 to 4 minutes.

7. Carefully remove from the heat and let rest for 5 minutes. Have spoons ready, because warm banana boats are a bit messy!

Tortilla Delights

Tortilla dessert packs are a camping favorite. They are super easy to make, and each camper can chef it up and make his or her own packet to suit. Mark each packet with the camper's name, or you could end up with some camp food fights.

It's pretty much impossible to mess up tortilla packs. It is, however, a good idea to remind campers not to load the tortillas with too much of the filling ingredients. If overloaded, Tortilla Delights become almost too messy to eat.

MAKES: As many as needed, or until ingredients are gone | **PREP TIME:** 15 to 20 minutes for a small group including kids | **GRILL TIME:** 15 minutes | **REST TIME:** 5 minutes

Foil needed: 1 nonstick grilling roll

flour tortillas, 1 per person (I find that 8-inch tortillas work out well, but any size is fine)

1 jar peanut butter

1 bag miniature marshmallows (8 ounces)

1 (12-ounce) bag chocolate chips

1. Give each person a piece of aluminum foil large enough to fully cover a filled tortilla.

2. Pass out the tortillas.

3. Have each person spread peanut butter on a tortilla, then add marshmallows and chocolate chips.

4. Carefully roll up the tortilla and place on the foil, seam-side down. Wrap the foil up and around to cover completely.

5. Place the foil packs over low heat on the grill or to the edge of the embers.

6. Heat until the tortillas are warm and the fillings are melted, usually around 15 minutes over a low heat source.

7. Let rest for 5 minutes, double-checking that the filled tortillas are cool enough to handle and eat.

Quick Tip: Be sure to buy soft, bendable flour tortillas for this dessert. If you find that your tortillas are stiff, you can warm them briefly in a microwave to soften them for rolling. Or if you are on a camping trip and don't have access to a microwave, sandwich tortillas between lightly moistened paper towels and set over the embers for a minute or so. Only warm 3 or 4 tortillas together at a time.

Corn Chip Bacon Treats

Combining the flavors of sugar and salt in desserts has been quite a delightful trend, I think. My cat thinks so, too. I bought a chocolate candy bar that had potato chips baked in, and the next morning I found a chewed-up wrapper on the kitchen floor and no candy bar to be found. Yes, my cat ate my gourmet chocolate bar.

Since even the cat loves salty-sweet flavors, I've been experimenting with foil packs using this combination of flavors. My favorites so far are corn chips with sugar and maple syrup. Corn Chip Bacon Treats are nice for a couple's evening around the campfire or for a group of kids making buddy packs to share.

MAKES: 2 servings | **PREP TIME:** 5 minutes | **GRILL TIME:** 13 minutes | **REST TIME:** 5 minutes
Foil needed: 2 (12 x 12-inch) pieces

1 cup corn chips
1 tablespoon light brown sugar
½ tablespoon butter

1 tablespoon maple syrup
2 slices bacon, crisply fried

1. Place the corn chips in the center of a foil piece and sprinkle the brown sugar over them.

2. Cut the butter in pea-size bits and distribute evenly over the chips.

3. Drizzle the maple syrup over the chips, then break the bacon into small bits and sprinkle over the chips.

4. Cover with the second piece of foil and seal on all sides.

5. Grill over medium-high heat for 5 minutes, then flip the pack over and grill for 8 more minutes.

6. Carefully remove from the grill. Let rest for 5 minutes, use a knife to vent the pack, and then peel back the edges of the foil to serve.

Fun Fact: My inspiration for corn chip bacon dessert was pig candy—thick slices of bacon with pecans and a sugar coating or glazing. This treat originated in the South and is especially popular with the barbecue competition crowd.

Cherry Pound Cake

This is my favorite campfire dessert. I love both pound cake and cherries, and when you add a little crunchy almond flavor and heat, you've got a dessert that will put a big smile on your face.

MAKES: 1 serving | **PREP TIME:** 5 minutes | **GRILL TIME:** 10 minutes | **REST TIME:** serve immediately

Foil needed: 1 (12 x 12-inch) nonstick piece

2 tablespoons almond butter

1¾-inch-thick slice frozen pound cake

1¼ cups canned cherry pie filling

1. Spread the almond butter on one side of the frozen pound cake slice.

2. Place on the aluminum foil, almond-butter side down, and spoon the cherries on top of the cake.

3. Pull the foil up and around the cake, leaving a bit of air space above the cherries.

4. Seal the top of the foil, then roll up both ends and crunch to seal.

5. Grill over medium-high heat for 10 minutes, turning at around 7 minutes.

6. Remove from the heat, carefully open, and serve.

Quick Tip: This recipe is pretty forgiving. You can use peanut butter instead of almond butter, and it's fine to try different types of fruit pie filling. You can even freeze those little sponge cake dessert shells to use in place of pound cake. All the variations are yummy, but I happen to like the combination of pound cake and cherries the best.

ABOUT THE AUTHOR

Cyndi Allison has been grilling and smoking since she was 12 years old. She started her blog, *Barbecue Master*, so that she could share recipes, tips, and reviews with family and friends. The blog gathered a following, and Cyndi began writing about outdoor cooking for a wider audience. When Cyndi is not grilling, she enjoys water sports, photography, and reading.